D1432986

MARX ON MONEY

MARX ON MONEY

SUZANNE DE BRUNHOFF

Translated by
Maurice J. Goldbloom

Preface by
Duncan K. Foley

URIZEN BOOKS, New York

This little book is a guide to Marx's views on money. It is a
point of access to ideas that have been much neglected in
twentieth-century debates on monetary theory and policy,
but provide, I think, valuable and plausible scientific alternatives
to the views that have dominated these debates.

The first thing a student of money notices is that in a monetary
economy the movements of money and commodities are in-
tertwined. At the level of the individual transaction some means
of payment moves in one direction and some commodity moves
in the opposite direction. The theoretical question then arises as
to which is the determining factor. Does the movement of money
determine the movement of commodities or the movement of
commodities determine the movement of money? Even if we
come to acknowledge a large measure of mutual determination
between the movements of money and commodities this question still provides the starting point for theories of money, and in
the end we will want to know from our theory which aspect is the
primary determining factor.

Consider for example the early form of the Quantity Theory of
Money. Since in every transaction a certain amount of money
changes places with commodities having a certain price, it is
clear that the total money price of commodities that a given
quantity of money can exchange for in a period is proportional
to the average number of times each unit of money moves in the
period, its velocity. This identity is the quantity equation of
money. The quantity theory asserts that all existing money participates equally in this circulation, so that the existing quantity
of money, and velocity, which depends on social and technical
factors outside the monetary sphere, determine the total price of
commodities exchanged in a period. In this theory the proximate
determinant of changes in the amounts of commodities exchanged is the effort of individuals to acquire or get rid of
money. The quantity theory usually argues that in long-run
equilibrium the money prices of commodities will adjust propor-
tionately to the quantity of existing money, so that the actual
quantities of commodities exchanged in the long-run equilibrium

are determined by nonmonetary factors like tastes and technology. Still it is clear that the starting point of the early quantity theory is the idea that movements of money determine movements of commodities. Keynes and those who adopt his monetary theory by and large take up a similar, though somewhat modified position. Changes in asset prices, interest rates, and, as a consequence, in spending within Keynes' theoretical framework are the result of the attempts of individual wealth-holders to adjust their holdings of money to some desired level. Again, changes in commodity flows are in large part determined by monetary changes.

As this book makes clear, Marx started from the opposite view that the movement of commodities is largely determined outside the monetary sphere, and that movements of money in most cases are determined by those commodity movements. Marx thus emphasizes a view of money as a medium through which commodity exchange takes place, a medium that transmits, but in most instances does not create, impulses of spending that originate outside itself. Units of money are moved by the exchange of commodities as molecules of water are displaced by a wave propagating through a pond. This general point of view is well illustrated, as de Brunhoff shows in the first part of this book, by Marx's discussion of the quantity equation, on which he bases his law of circulation. Not only the quantities of commodities produced and exchanged and the transactions velocity of money, but also the money prices of commodities are taken by Marx as determined outside the circulation process. It is the quantity of circulating money in Marx's view that adjusts to satisfy the quantity equation, a sharp reversal of the quantity theory interpretation.

This view that money is primarily a transmitting medium rather than an active disturbing element in the economy also carries over to Marx's complex and incomplete discussion of credit and interest. Here interest appears as a simple quantitative division of total profit, with no power to determine the rate of profit or the rate of investment. This is in sharp contrast to Keynes' view that the rate of interest is an important determining factor in investment through its influence on the "marginal efficiency of capital" (the profit rate on current investment).

Despite the fact that Marx sees movements of money as primarily determined by movements of commodities, he does not argue that money is "neutral" or "a veil," or that it "does not matter." For example, Marx emphasizes that the existence of money and the possibility of hoarding are preconditions for a general crisis of overproduction in a capitalist economy. This is one instance where Marx's unified treatment of "macroeconomics" and "microeconomics" is clearly advantageous. Marx never separates the theoretical terms in which he discusses the reproduction of particular capitals from the terms in which he discusses the reproduction of the capitalist system as a whole. At each level Marx explicitly analyzes the role and movement of money and makes clear its qualitative importance. In this way he avoids the theoretical embarrassment of having distinct and incompatible theories of macroeconomics and microeconomics. Modern bourgeois economics begins with a theory of the firm and the household which abstracts from the existence of money and assumes that commodities can be exchanged directly for each other without the intervention of money. This type of theory leads to a notion of equilibrium for the economy as a whole that rules out crises of overproduction and widespread unemployment of labor. To explain these important features of capitalist economic development bourgeois economics adopts a quite different theory, developed from the work of Keynes, which is unfortunately inconsistent with the bourgeois microeconomic theory of the firm and household in several ways. A leading theoretical problem in modern bourgeois economics is to reconcile these two theories with each other in an appropriate way. Marx avoids this problem by creating a unified treatment of individual capital and the capitalist system as a whole, a treatment which at every level acknowledges the role that money plays. This feature should recommend the study of his theory of money to modern students of monetary problems.

Marx's treatment of money, which as Suzanne de Brunhoff

shows, represents his reading and criticism of the major writers on money available to him, offers a consistent scientific explanation of the major phenomena of monetary economies. Furthermore, this explanation is distinctly different from the dominant positions in twentieth-century monetary theory, and yields different explanations of particular historical events. An instance of this is the question of the degree to which the monetary policy of the state can create or moderate crises in the accumulation of capital. Keynes' analysis of this question, which concludes that within broad limits monetary policy can alter the rate of investment and determine aggregate demand, is at sharp variance with the presumption we arrive at on the basis of Marx's discussion, which limits the effects of monetary policy to the sphere of money and credit, and sees monetary policy having its major impact on the concentration of capitals in periods of crisis.

To discover and formulate these differences in a form sufficiently precise for use in statistical and historical studies is a substantial theoretical task. Marx's writings on money remain in a "pre-model" stage, and it will be necessary for us to bring this theoretical position to the point of exact expression in a series of models. De Brunhoff's work in this book represents an invaluable first investigation of this problem on which much further work can be built.

As de Brunhoff shows, the question of money is one of the central organizing threads in Marx's analysis of capitalist production. In the course of outlining Marx's thoughts on money this book provides very valuable insights into the structure of his study of capitalism and throws light on certain very difficult questions of Marxist interpretation. A good example is the vexed question of the starting point for *Capital*, the question of why Marx began his studies of capitalism with an analysis of commodity and money forms. *Marx on Money* provides an illuminating discussion on this problem. De Brunhoff's method of analysis also gives us a complete overview of the structure and argument of the three volumes of *Capital* taken together.

Most modern monetary theory has been undertaken with the explicit aim of improving state monetary policies in modern capitalism. This study of Marx's monetary theory shows how little Marx was motivated in this direction. In monetary theory, as in most of his analytical work on capitalism, Marx seeks first of all to discover the objective determinants of social phenomena, the laws of motion of the system. A correct understanding of the relation of money to the production and exchange of commodities, which is clearly the aim of Marx's contribution, is a precondition for a sensible evaluation of the potential and performance of monetary policy in capitalist society. But Marx's approach does not necessarily lead directly to results that will help monetary policy-makers in their problems.

This does not mean that Marx's monetary theory has no political consequences. In advanced capitalist societies the monetary mechanism is closely bound up with the State, and political struggles often focus around monetary policy and management. Inflation and unemployment are in advanced capitalist societies major issues over which class struggle is fought out. Workers who have again and again been asked and forced to accept lower or less rapidly rising wages or unemployment as part of a national policy against inflation can testify to this. These issues are intimately connected to monetary theory and policy. A scientific understanding of the nature and consequences of monetary policy is necessary for a correct strategy of political struggle and debate over these questions of national economic policy. Those who are engaged in these struggles on the side of the working class can only be weakened by relying on a monetary analysis adopted from Keynes or other bourgeois economists to the extent that this analysis is incorrect. A correct theory of money firmly based on the principles of the materialist conception of history is essential. Marx worked to formulate such a theory in its basics, and Suzanne de Brunhoff in this book takes the first steps toward recovering and completing that theory. *Marx on Money* is in this sense an important intellectual contribution to political struggle.

—Duncan K. Foley

CONTENTS

t first glance one does not know what to make of the analyses of money which appear at the beginning of *Capital*. Marx began his study of capitalist production with an analysis of commodities, exchanges, and circulation in terms of a process of commodity production without socially determined conditions: money would at first appear not to have a capitalist context. Why did Marx not rather follow Ricardo, who proposed to choose a commodity standard based on the social conditions of commodity production?[2] Schumpeter thought the theory of money one of the weak points of *Capital*, and considered Marx inferior to Ricardo on this question.

The lack of attention given to this part of *Capital* seems to have represented an acceptance of Marx's surprising approach. For some Marxists money, without any scientific meaning, has become a symbol of the "reification" of social relations between private producers. Others have gone along with the letter of Marx's analyses without looking for logical, rather than historical, reasons why they are at the beginning of *Capital*. But this is not due to the fact that a commercial economy preceded capitalism. Otherwise Marx's analysis would have been altogether different. It would have taken account of the fact that capitalism is still a commercial economy, and linked the monetary character of money to the requirements of the form of production. It would, for example, have taken up Ricardo's suggestion that the average proportions of labor and capital determine the choice of a money, so that money would be the standard commodity of a particular form of commodity production.

In contrast Marx, before examining credit under capitalism, gives us a study of money which disregards the organic composition of capital. It is this abstract study of the monetary characteristics of money which leads into the analysis of the financing of capitalist production. Not only is money studied in abstraction from capitalism, but its place at the beginning of *Capital* is not dependent on the priority of pre-capitalist economies. The question is how this method, doubly separated from history, makes it possible to understand the economic role of money.

Marx knows that his analysis differs profoundly from that of other economists, and he gives the reason. "It is one of the chief failings of classical economy that it has never succeeded, by means of its analysis of commodities, and, in particular, of their value, in discovering that form under which value becomes exchange-value. . . . We consequently find that economists, who are thoroughly agreed as to labour time being the measure of the magnitude of value, have the most strange and contradictory ideas of money, the perfected form of the general equivalent. This is seen in a striking manner when they treat of banking, where the commonplace definitions of money will no longer hold water."[3]

To determine the nature of money, the point of departure must then be a "deductive" analysis, without regard to its concrete forms and its role in capitalism. This should enable us to avoid two errors which hinder our understanding of the role of money in capitalism, the confusion of money with commodities and of money with capital.

To put together the meaning of this theory of money, which first appears in the initial pages of the first volume and is the framework for the notes on credit in Part 3 of Volume II, is to read *Capital* as a whole. L. Althusser[4] has shown the differences between Marx's theories in *Capital* and those of the classical economists, thereby furnishing a basis for understanding how they all fit together. A misunderstanding of the premises of Marx's theory of money may prevent one from understanding everything that follows, especially the relation between money and credit. In this way a large part of the analyses of the financing of accumulation and the role of credit, contained in Parts 2 and 3, is lost. (Thus H. Denis, who supports a labor-value theory of money much closer to Ricardo than to Marx, has little to say about them.[5]) Or else these analyses are used in the examination of credit and banks, but without being organically linked to the theory of money in Part 1. This disassociation has probably been one of the reasons for the overestimation of the role of "finance capital," in the manner of Hilferding. In either case it has both reflected and led to a poor understanding of the relation that exists between the different parts of *Capital*.

But what is the point of thus illuminating the coherence of a theory if that theory has no relevance? Have there not been such radical changes in monetary systems in the past half century that, when one discusses money, one is talking about something entirely different from what Marx was dealing with? Even an explanation solely in terms of the "history of ideas" would then risk being full of misinterpretations.

But this objection is not valid, because the content of a theory of money does not depend mainly on the "particular kind of money" used (metallic money or convertible paper or inconvertible paper). What needs to be explained is the economic basis for the existence of money, not merely as a measure of value and a means of circulation, but as the object of a specific demand even when its predominant form is inconvertible paper. This is the monetary characteristic of money which is the basis of its economic existence: "we cannot get rid of money even by abolishing gold and silver and legal tender instruments."[6] Marx discovered this eighty years before Keynes. It is necessary to recall how and why.

PART ONE

THE MARXIST THEORY OF MONEY

A. A "GENERAL" THEORY OF MONEY

The Marxist theory of money interests us primarily because of its integration with the theory of the capitalist form of production. Since money is part of the machinery of capitalism, its role is determined by its functions within the entire pattern of capitalist economic relations. According to Marx money is "a social relation of production"; therefore, under capitalism, it is part of the capitalist system of relations of production. But it participates in them in its special fashion, by existing in the form of money, and the monetary problem consists precisely in knowing the meaning of this strange existence as money, inseparable but distinct from the other relations characteristic of capitalism. Often forgotten or made parenthetical in the analyses "in real terms" of our contemporaries, money suddenly reappears, incapable of reduction to the other "variables" of the system. Handed over to specialists, it disappears again, but only after inconveniencing everyone and disrupting a good number of plans and projects. An analysis of money as an integral part of capitalist relationships of production can offer an explanation of the fundamental relations of adjustment and maladjustment between the "real" and the "monetary" in terms of the financing of accumulation and its cyclical metamorphoses. But it is not enough to formulate a *theory of the specific form of money*, i.e., of those monetary phenomena which persist or recur in contradistinction to other economic phenomena.

Hence a theory of money applicable to the capitalist system must be subsumed under a theory of money in general, valid for every monetary economy; in other words, a general theory of money. And Marx's examination of this question bears fruit in the *Marxist theory of money* expounded in the first section of Part 1 of *Capital*. Thus Marx considers it necessary to begin with a study of money *in its general aspect, independent of the capitalist form of production* in order, among other things, to determine its role *in* the capitalist form of production.

This method can be disconcerting if one has misunderstood the purpose of a theory of money and does not see that to start with money as it functions in the capitalist form of production is, while seeming faithful to Marxism, to misinterpret Marx's theory of money as a description of a "monetary relationship" separate from the capitalist relation of production, and to make the relation between money and credit incomprehensible. Thus it is wrong to regard the first section of *Capital* as the elaboration of a hypothetical structure[1] in which the common sense views or vulgar concepts of money and commodities become elements of a theoretical analysis, leaving the problem of money to be resolved elsewhere by the theory of production. This makes Section 1 represent a sort of theory of the non-theory of money. Such an interpretation is erroneous; in the first section of *Capital*, Marx gives a general theory of the circulation of commodities and money. The causes of this error lie in a poor understanding of the structure of the capitalist form of production, which combines economic elements differing in nature, origin, and manner of action; its consequence is to aggravate this misunderstanding. One becomes unable to see how the *general* laws of monetary circulation continue to function in the capitalist form of production where there is a *special* monetary circulation, that of credit.

Another aspect of the same error consists in accepting as complete the partial account of the functions of money analyzed by Marx in Chapter III of Part I in the first volume of *Capital*, when only the exposition as a whole constitutes the theory of money. This point will be discussed further, but it is necessary here to point out the inadequacy of such an analysis as that of Hilferding. He begins his study of *Finance Capital*[2] with three chapters which seem to follow the order of the presentation in *Capital:* 1) The need for money; 2) Money in the process of circulation; 3) Money as means of payment, credit money. But Hilferding devotes himself to discussing inconvertible paper and credit money, contemporary forms of money linked to the capitalist form of production, without first explaining the ensemble of the functions of money which in their entirety constitute the general theory of money. Money as an instrument of hoarding does not appear in the first chapters of his study. This omission in regard to money in general has grave consequences, since the monetary theory of credit *involves* a knowledge of the role of hoarding. Hilferding's error has the same roots as the one referred to above. To want to describe the functions of money under capitalist conditions without first stating the entire general theory of money is to miss their meaning.

Nevertheless Marx gave numerous indications of his method. They can be grouped under three heads:

1) The circulation of commodities and money is characteristic of "commodity production," defined entirely by general social relationship: "private exchange presupposes private production." Since money is the expression of a general relationship of exchange between private economic agents, "the money-economy is common to all commodity production."[3]

One may ask if the notion of commodity production is not the result of a simple combination of the analysis of exchange and the theory of value, a combination so general that it cannot serve as the starting-point for the study of capitalist production. But the science of production requires an appropriate analysis of monetary exchanges if it is not to find itself obstructed by a money whose economic status has not been previously defined. The capitalist economy is necessarily a monetary economy. And only if one assigns a definite economic existence to money can one separate the barter economy from the monetary economy completely and without harm to the study of production. Then one will see that hoarding meets a need and represents a conversion of value by private economic agents, marking the dividing line between the monetary and barter economies in such a way that it is impossible to analyze the equilibrium of exchanges in capitalist production in "real" terms as if money had no economic role. The preliminary analysis of monetary exchanges is closely linked to the grand design of *Capital*.

2) Consequently, "It is . . . wrong to attempt to derive the specific properties and functions which characterise money as money and commodities as commodities from their quality as capital. . . ."[4]

3) That is why it is necessary to begin with the simple circulation of metallic money in constructing the (general) theory of money, rather than to start with credit in the capitalist form of production. A historical reason is given by Marx in *Capital*: ". . . this is the historical order; credit money plays only a very

minor role, or none at all, during the first epoch of capitalist production."

Nevertheless I think that the principal reason is this: "In the
second place, the necessity of this order is demonstrated
theoretically by the fact that everything of a critical nature which
Tooke and others hitherto expounded in regard to the circulation
of credit-money compelled them to hark back again and again
to the question of what would be the aspect of the matter if nothing but metal-money were in circulation."[5] On several occasions
Marx returns to this point, as when he criticizes MacLeod for
wanting to derive money in general from its most advanced
form, credit, or when he indicates that Tooke and Fullarton confuse money with capital or with commodities because they "do
not first of all examine money in its abstract form in which it develops within the framework of simple commodity circulation and
grows out of the relations of commodities in circulation."[6]

Marx considers it necessary to begin with "simple," i.e.,
abstract, circulation in order to understand money in the
capitalist form of production. Only thus can one construct a
general theory of money. The simplification of starting from
metallic money is nothing but "the good abstraction" necessary
to determine the specific character of every "monetary relation."

It is necessary to be specific on this point, in order not to be
the victim of a new paradox. In simple circulation one studies
the ebb and flow of money in relation to other commodities; this
abstraction has the appearance of a visible datum, with all the
brilliance and solidity of metal. In contrast, the network of debts
and credits which Marx rejects as a starting-point for the
analysis of money, forms an immaterial circuit in which reciprocal obligations and rights confront and counterbalance one
another. Why does "the good abstraction" take as its initial object the metallic material of money and not some of the elements
already spontaneously abstracted by the very process of
monetary circulation? In another form, it is the same question of
the starting-point which is raised anew when Marx relates credit
to the capitalist form of production and differentiates it from the
general concept of money, valid for all commodity production.
But the answer to this question now requires that we return to

the reason why the specific form of money follows from the monetary role of gold.

Metallic circulation serves as a starting point because "the simple commodity form is . . . the germ of the money form,"[7] and because to discover the genesis of the money-commodity form is to show how a commodity-metal becomes the money-commodity. Gold is able to play the role of money in relation to other commodities because it has already played the role of commodity in relation to them. This is the best-known point in Marx's exposition. It is unquestionably a necessary link, but if one isolates it from what follows, one still does not see the special character of the money form. The commodity excluded from the series of commodities as "the general equivalent or money" simultaneously excludes all other commodities from the character of general equivalent. It has a socially validated monopoly of equivalence, and this is what characterizes its social function as money; *moreover, it preserves and reproduces itself incessantly in its distinct form.* Without clarity on this basic point, the idea of money as commodity can give birth to the opposite idea, that of gold as a simple symbol of the value of commodities. For if gold remains a commodity like the others, then inversely "Every commodity is immediately money"[8] and the monetary privilege assigned to gold appears arbitrary and unfounded. Since the inherent measure of value is labor-time, money could be a simple record of rights acquired in return for labor-time furnished for the production of different commodities. This, says Marx, was Gray's theory, deduced from his incomplete and therefore incorrect analysis of commodities. A complete analysis of commodities should include the genesis of the money form, i.e., the transformation of one commodity into a general equivalent *distinct* from all commodities. It should cover the process of the formation of money as something different from commodities and set off against them. Without this, every commodity would be money and all money a simple commodity, so that there would be neither money nor commodity production in which "private exchange presupposes private production."

The historical reason why the theory of money should consider metallic money first is thus logically subordinate to the theoretical reason, which establishes the necessity for money in all commodity production by starting with the genesis of the form "general equivalent or money." This idea of Marx constitutes the essential difference between the Marxist theory of money and the theories not only of MacLeod and Fullarton, but of Ricardo as well.

Nevertheless Ricardo makes use of the same premises as Marx; he begins by the study of gold as money commodity, determining its value in the same way as that of other commodities. "To begin with, Ricardo determines the value of gold and silver, like the value of all other commodities, by the quantity of labour-time materialised in them. The value of other commodities is measured in terms of the precious metals, which are commodities of a determinate value."[9]

One sees a great similarity, and it is tempting to think that Marx began his examination of money by an analysis of metallic money in order to combine the tradition of the money commodity with the theory of value as labor, as Ricardo had previously done. But such an interpretation would make it impossible to understand why Ricardo, according to Marx, showed himself unfaithful to his own premises, or why Marx criticizes the error of those who treat money as a simple commodity, determining its value as a commodity without understanding what differentiates money from commodities. In *Capital* the initial simplification effected by the examination of metallic circulation is not a return to Richardo's premises. Rather, it permits Marx to transform the import of these premises, and to abstract the special meaning of money which differentiates it from commodities, at the point at which it at first appears impossible to show that essential difference, since money as a metal commodity is of the same nature as other commodities. It is because "The difficulty lies, not in comprehending that money is a commodity, but in discovering how, why, and by what means a commodity becomes money,"[10] that the necessary starting-point for the general theory of money is the study of "simple" circulation, a fruitful simplification or abstraction.

Thus the Marxist theory of money starts with the identification of the "general equivalent form or money" which differentiates one commodity from all others and all commodities from money. This is really a general theory of money, since the form thus analyzed is what gives all money, in every "monetary economy," its principal meaning. But a second step is necessary to describe the relationship between this money "form" and the multiple functions and aspects of money. The latter should all be like forms of the money form. But the relationship established by Marx is not at all that which could exist between an "essential" character of money and the "phenomena" which express it. All the forms of the "general equivalent form" which he analyzes are functions of money which complement one another, different yet necessarily linked with each other, *which only in combination preserve and reproduce the general equivalent form.* To omit a single one, or to misplace it in relation to the others, is to put in doubt both the specific character of money and the general meaning of the monetary theory. In other words, only a complete theory of the functions of money makes it possible to completely define the specific form of money and achieve a *general* monetary theory. That is why the functions of money now need to be analyzed in relation to one another and in an order fixed by the requirements of the complete definition of the money form—the same order followed by Marx in Chapter III of the first section of *Capital.*

B. A "COMPLETE" THEORY OF MONEY

1) "The Measure of Value"; 2) "The Medium of Circulation"; 3) "Money." These are the three major points analyzed in succession by Marx. One is immediately struck by the discussion of the third point under the heading "Money" in a chapter entirely devoted to money and its various functions. The functions of "measure of value" and "medium of circulation" nevertheless have no meaning independent of the "money form or general equivalent." But they do not always imply the "presence in person" of money as a tangible embodiment of the general equivalent form. Thus the order followed is a progression organized in terms of the "money form" which determines all the connected steps, including the final appearance of money "in the full sense of the

term." But it is only *at the end of the three steps that "the economic existence" of money is fully defined*, although its character of general equivalent is the animating principle of all its functions and their articulation.

a. Money, Measure of Value

Money as "measure of value" or "the money form as the price of commodities" is deduced directly from the origin of the general equivalent. "Gold becomes the *measure of value* because the exchange-value of *all* commodities is measured in gold, as expressed in the relation of a definite quantity of gold and a definite quantity of commodity containing equal amounts of labour-time."[11] What will turn up later as, in Wicksell's words, "the monetary problem *par excellence*," that of knowing how to determine "the general price level" as opposed to the relative prices determined in the exchange of products among themselves, *does not exist here as a monetary problem*. There are no "circulating use values" whose respective utilities confront one another, independent of monetary prices dependent on a money of undetermined value. Only commodities circulate; since they cannot be exchanged immediately among themselves, their circulation implies money.[12] Commodities enter into circulation with a price and money with a value; the "monetary problem *par excellence*" has been posed and resolved even before the entrance of money onto the scene, in the transition from the "relative" form of value to the general equivalent form,[13] in such a way that the fixing of monetary prices is identical with the emergence of money form.

Nevertheless the money form implies the production of money as a commodity. And if the value of gold (the labor-time needed for its production) changes while the values of all commodities remain the same, then, all other things being equal, the general price level changes. If the labor-time necessary to produce a given quantity of gold doubles, monetary prices will fall by a half—first those of commodities bought by the producers-sellers of gold, then bit by bit those of all commodities as their prices adapt themselves to their relative values, which by hypothesis do not change during the process. There is thus a modification of the *monetary prices alone*, due to the change in the relative value of gold as a commodity. Does this bring one back to Wicksell's monetary problem and what our contemporaries call the "dichotomy" of the "real" sector (commodities by themselves) and the "monetary" sector (commodities in relation to money)? No, by hypothesis, since according to Marx money is a special commodity transformed into money. But *at this stage of the analysis* money remains rooted in the exchange of equivalent commodities, and Marx's analysis differs from that of Ricardo only in his insistence on the uniqueness of the money form.

The possible deviation of the *price* of a commodity (its exchange-ratio with money) from the *value* of that commodity, which does not vary if the necessary labor expended in its production remains the same, represents the specific difference in the ratio of the *money form* to *equivalent* commodities.

But although price, being the exponent of the magnitude of a commodity's value, is the exponent of its exchange-ratio with money, it does not follow that the exponent of this exchange-ratio is necessarily the exponent of the commodity's value. Suppose two equal quantities of socially necessary labor to be respectively represented by one quarter of wheat and £ 2 (nearly ½ oz. of gold), £ 2 is the expression in money of the magnitude of the value of the quarter of wheat, or is its price. If now circumstances allow of this price being raised to £ 3, or compel it to be reduced to £ 1, then although £ 1 and £ 3 may be too small or too great properly to express the magnitude of the wheat's value, nevertheless they are its prices, for they are, in the first place, the form under which its value appears, i.e., money; and in the second place, the exponents of its exchange-ratio with money. . . . The possibility, therefore, of quantitative incongruity between price and magnitude of value, or the deviation of the former from the latter, is inherent in the price-form itself.[14]

The distinction Marx makes between the money and commodity forms, and its consequences for the relation between the price and value of a commodity, cannot be assimilated to the dichotomy between "relative prices" in the "real" sector and

"monetary prices." That dichotomy has reference to the determination of all prices and all values by markets (supply and demand of goods and money). At this stage in Marx's exposition,
there is no examination of the relations between markets of different types, but only a study of the general conditions of the
circulation of commodities, including money. In its role of "measure of value," the money commodity is "neutral" in relation to
the exchange value of commodities. But there is no place here
for the idea of the dichotomy of the two sectors, attributed to the
"classical" economists, or for the approach which attempts to
suppress that dichotomy by postulating an interplay of "demand" for money and the "supply" of it. In *Capital*, the problem
of the distinction between price and value, so far as it concerns
the value relationships of the gold price and the commodity
value of the commodity, is simultaneously posed and resolved
by the definition of the money form. So far as it concerns the
market price of commodity values, it cannot be resolved or even
posed in the study of simple circulation, since it has reference to
the analysis of markets in a capitalist society. Hence the problem of divergence between money prices and relative values of
commodities is not "the monetary problem *par excellence*." The
problem here, that of the money form and its solution as previously noted, does not depend on the way different markets are
interconnected, but on the exchange of equivalents and the
coming into existence of a general equivalent. "Price, in its general meaning, is but value in the form of money."[15]

The divergence between price and value does not, then, prevent money from serving as *measure of value*. That function depends *at one and the same time* on the equivalence of commodities and money and on their formal difference. The conditions under which it operates involve their own general limits;
one aspect of these is the divergence between price and value.

The role of money as a measure of value involves two complementary determinations. Since the starting-point of the
analysis of money is the exchange of equivalent commodities,
gold as a commodity "has a potentially variable value." To give
it a fixed value would be to destroy the basis of the monetary
function of gold as measure of value, its nature as a commodity,

and to attribute to it a mysterious power to make commodities commensurate with one another. Nevertheless, the same reason which makes it necessary to attribute a variable value to gold prevents it from having a price, i.e., serving as its own equivalent. If it did, it would remain one commodity among the others and lose its character of general equivalent and its function as measure of value. One sees why the order of arguments must be observed; in succession Marx discusses a "market price" of money as medium of circulation and then, in the analysis of credit, the price of money on a money market. But to speak of a price of *money as measure of value* would lead to confusion.

It is likewise to avoid this confusion that Marx *distinguishes* between the characteristics of gold as *measure of value* (its value varies with the circumstances under which it is produced) and those of gold as standard of price, where a weight of metal fixed by custom serves as a unit of measurement which permits the comparison of the prices of commodities with one another, whatever the variations in the value of gold. This distinction is very close to that made by Ricardo in his *Principles of Political Economy and Taxation.* But for Ricardo it is the hypothesis of the invariability of the monetary standard that determines the monetary character of a commodity whose value is variable like that of all other commodities. But for Marx, money is different from commodities even *before* being fixed as a standard.

In simple circulation, the standard of price has a "monetary price" fixed by convention.

A given weight of one of the precious metals, an ounce of gold, for instance, becomes officially divided into aliquot parts, with legally bestowed names, such as pound, dollar, etc. These aliquot parts, which henceforth serve as units of money, are then subdivided into other aliquot parts with legal names, such as shilling, penny, etc. But, both before and after these divisions are made, a definite weight of metal is the standard of metallic money. . . . The prices, or quantities of gold, into which the values of commodities are ideally changed, are therefore now expressed in the names of coins, or in the legally valid names of the subdivisions of the gold standard.

Hence, instead of saying: A quarter of wheat is worth an ounce gold; we say, it is worth £ 3 17s. 10½d.[16]

The name given a certain amount of gold, or "monetary price," serves as a unit of account. "The specific form which the exchange-value of commodities assumes is converted into *denominations of money*, by which their value is expressed. Money in turn becomes *money of account*."[17]

One will see under the following point (No. 2) that only the "monetary price" belongs to gold as standard unit of account, and that it has nothing to do with gold as measure of value, which cannot have a price. Every confusion between the different aspects of money, every exposition which disturbs the order indicated by Marx, has the effect of destroying the specific character of the money form, i.e., the very essence of the Marxist theory of money.

I shall return subsequently to the conventional character of the monetary standard, which implies state intervention. Marx repeatedly speaks of the monetary role of the state, whose significance it is necessary to define. But for that it is first necessary to know all the elements of the theory of money and arrange them in order. Moreover, it is difficult otherwise to understand why, in his theoretical explanations Marx omitted a large part of the considerations on the "money power" which are present in a fragment of the first draft version of *The Critique of Political Economy.*[18]

b. Money, Medium of Circulation

The distinction and necessary connection between the forms of money, presented in an irreversible order, explain the role of gold as medium of circulation once it has been established as the measure of value. On the one hand, money serves as the medium of circulation once it has been established as the measure of value and standard of price. On the other, in the development of the analysis, money as medium of circulation is not merely the manifestation but the *practical* guarantee of the role of money as measure of value. The fixing of prices permits the comparison of commodities to be exchanged; it does not guarantee their effective circulation, that is, their sale in exchange for a sum of money which makes it possible to continue with purchases and sales. Only circulation, in which money effectively replaces commodities, gives the fixing of prices its full significance. The first function of money is the condition for the second, but the second is the necessary complement of the first. Without this connection, money would have only a purely functional character, as medium of circulation, or a purely "ideal" character, as unit of account. The initial measurement of value by gold as a commodity would change nothing, since it implies only a single initial exchange. In a peculiar phrase, Marx says that "the sphere of circulation has an opening through which gold (or the material of money generally) enters into it as a commodity"[19] with a value established at a given moment. But nevertheless not all the stock of gold produced and sold, which "enters in," circulates.

"It is clear that, if gold and silver themselves have value, quite irrespective of all other laws of circulation, only a definite quantity of gold and silver can circulate as the equivalent of a given aggregate value of commodities."[20] And the quantity of gold that can actually circulate depends on the actual exchanges of commodities. Here Marx departs radically from Ricardo, to whom he was just so close.

New characteristics appear belonging to money as instrument of circulation. The quantity of gold that circulates is a variable dependent on prices and the volume and speed of transactions. The first function of money has as a condition the variability of its value; the second implies the variability of the quantity that circulates. The two conditions are different.

"The law, that the quantity of the circulating medium is determined by the sum of the prices of the commodities circulating and the average velocity of currency, may also be stated as follows: given the sum of the values of commodities, and the average rapidity of their metamorphoses, the quantity of precious metal current as money depends on the value of that precious metal."[21]

But the reciprocal is not true. "Any scholarly investigation of the relation between the volume of means of circulation and movements in commodity-prices must assume that the value of the monetary material is given."[22]

The value of money varies in its production and initial sale (function No. 1), but as the instrument of circulation it has by hypothesis a given value, while its quantity is variable. The difference between the total stock of gold and the amount which circulates is absorbed by hoarding. (Third function of money, to be examined later.) These points form the basis for Marx's refutation of the Quantity Theory of Money. Thus the intrinsic connection between these functions rules out not only their separation but their presentation in any old order and their confusion with one another. Hence the metamorphoses of money in circulation do not raise any question about the value of gold as general equivalent and measure of value; they affect only the instrument of circulation. Minted into coins and transformed into currency, gold can, in circulating, demonetize itself; it loses its weight of metal and becomes the shadow of its own metallic substance. This loss of its matter explains the difference between the "monetary price" and the "market price" of gold;[23] the public mint always produces coins according to the same standard but the pieces in circulation, used and clipped, weigh less than their name indicates. Having become lighter, they only correspond to a smaller quantity of gold, and the monetary price is less than the market price for the same quantity. "The weight of gold fixed upon as the standard of prices deviates from the weight that serves as the circulating medium, and the latter thereby ceases any longer to be a real equivalent of the commodities whose prices it realizes."[24]

Nevertheless, this demonetization of the currency does not detract from the dependence of the instrument of circulation on the true value of the gold. The quantity which actually circulates remains distinct from the total quantity of gold, and the course of its circulation continues to be determined by the value relationships between money as general equivalent and the prices of commodities. The modification of the coins affects only the special form of the medium of circulation.

Nevertheless the process of dematerialization continues in the course of circulation, where gold can be replaced by "relatively valueless things, such as paper bills," which are fiat money with compulsory currency (as distinguished from banknotes, which are credit money). It should then seem that the instrument of circulation, completely detached from its metallic substance, also serves as the measure of the value of commodities, with a value of its own. In that case the distinction between the functions of money would end up in a complete separation, depriving money of its initial significance and leaving it only a value dependent on its quantity. Instead of having a given value and a variable quantity as an instrument of circulation, paper money has a quantity determined by the amount printed, irrespective of the requirements of circulation, and a value inversely proportional to that quantity. What Marx called "the inherent laws of circulation," based on the role of the money commodity, appear to be abolished when the medium of circulation, with no intrinsic value, depends on governmental decisions which fix the amount issued. Marx's refutation of the quantitativism of Ricardo would lose its general character if paper money were excepted from it.

According to Ricardo, given the amount of money, the value of money depends on the relation between its volume and the volume of commodities; this applies to all money, including gold. If the sum of the values of commodities in circulation diminishes, or if the amount of gold produced increases, there is too much gold in circulation in relation to the value in exchange of the same volume of commodities, and hence in relation to the value of gold. The gold in circulation devalues itself in relation to its own value, and commodities are evaluated in a metal with a value less than that of gold. Their prices rise, because the amount of gold in circulation exceeds the amount in the initial state of equilibrium, and this increase absorbs the excess money. But the value relations between gold at the point of production and commodities remain altered. The fall of gold, which circulates below its cost of production, causes a decrease in its production and reduces the amount in circulation, which makes prices fall. At the end of this process, equilibrium (value of gold at the point of production—value of gold in circulation—value of commodities) is reestablished.[25] In the case of paper money, this can be done in a different way, if its issuance is restricted sufficiently by the state. Marx accepted this idea of Ricardo's in his criticism of Proudhon in *The Poverty of Philosophy*.

> *So long as there is a certain proportion observed between the requirements of circulation and the amount of money issued, be it paper, gold, platinum or copper money, there can be no question of a proportion to be observed between the intrinsic value (cost of production) and the nominal value of money. . . . Ricardo understood this truth so well that, after basing his whole system on value determined by labour time, and after saying: "Gold and silver, like all other commodities, are valuable only in proportion to the quantity of labour necessary to produce them, and bring them to market," he adds, nevertheless, that the value of* money *is not determined by the labour time its substance embodies, but by the law of supply and demand only.*[26]

Marx subsequently indicated that money has a relative scarcity which constitutes its value.

But the theses advanced in *The Poverty of Philosophy* are rejected and refuted in *Capital*. There, as H. Bartoli has shown, Marx integrates the value of money into his general economic theory. Since paper money does not lend itself well to that integration, can one nevertheless say with H. Bartoli[27] that Marx, resolutely anti-quantitativist in dealing with metallic money, returns to quantitativism when he analyzes paper money?

Several points make this questionable. (One must nevertheless recognize that Marx never explained them all clearly.) Following Tooke, Marx criticizes the confusion created by Ricardo in attributing the same economic role to all sorts of money—gold, fiat money, and banknotes—and holding that variations in the price level are determined by the variations in the total amount of money of all kinds. Marx says that if Ricardo fails to distinguish between the various kinds of money and their different forms, it is because he is obsessed by the role of the quantity of the medium of circulation.[28] Charles Rist summarized the monetary views of Ricardo in terms close to those of Marx: "The notion of quantity entirely dominates Ricardo's monetary theory; the price level depends on the amount of money, whether metal or paper. . . . Never prior to Ricardo had anyone formulated so simplified a theory of the relationship between money, whatever it was, and prices."[29]

Marx rejects this concept completely, not because he himself adheres to an exclusively "metallicist" concept of money, but because the idea of identifying fiat money and credit money with metallic money rests on a confusion of the different functions of money, reducing it to the single form of medium of circulation. Ricardo's mistake is that he "regards currency, the fluid form of money, in isolation."[30] The distinction Marx makes between paper fiat money and metallic money is a part of the basic distinction between money as measure of value and money as medium of circulation. Instead of tending toward a quantity theory of paper money, he seeks to get rid of quantity theory for all kinds of money. Marx completely rejects the Quantity Theory of Money; to accept it on a limited point would undermine the logic of his monetary theory.

That is why the analysis of the nature of paper money is included in that of the process of dematerialization of all circulating money, a process which also affects metal coins. The loss of metallic substance in circulation never results in reducing money to a mere medium of circulation. Rather, it is an indication of the functional difference between money as measure of value and money as instrument of circulation.

Nevertheless, the analysis of paper money is not entirely clear in *Capital*. Paper fiat money is without any doubt money. But it is hard to tell whether it is "false money," as Pareto was later to say, or true money whose monetary role is entirely derivative from that of gold. In either case, one can agree with Charles Rist that "The theory of paper money is to that of metallic money as in medicine the study of the pathology of an organ is to that of its normal anatomy and physiology."[31]

Marx describes a "pathological" effect of paper money when he says that the circulation of bills issued at will by the state "mechanically infringes by extraneous action" the laws of simple circulation.[32] He subsequently shows that in the end these laws nonetheless impose themselves, since paper money is only a symbol of gold and its circulation is in the last analysis regulated

by the need for metallic money. If the state issues too much
paper money in relation to the amount of gold it represents,
the paper money devalues itself and the rise of prices absorbs
the excess bills. "The effect would be the same as if an altera-
tion had taken place in the function of gold as a standard of
prices.[33]

Equilibrium reestablishes itself in terms of a given value for
monetary gold, which remains distinct from paper money. The
nominal increase in prices thus has no economic importance, in
the sense that it does not affect the primary determination of
prices. (In the same way, though for different reasons, Keynes
explains in the *Treatise on Money*[34] that if the quantity of money
is doubled, the level of prices is multiplied by two, but that this
relation is purely a phenomenon of equilibrium which has nothing to do with the economic process of the determination of the
price level.) According to Marx paper money is true money, related to gold as its symbol; i.e., the demonetization of the gold
replaced by paper implies a compensatory "monetization" of the
latter by the role gold plays indirectly.

But in another respect fiat money nevertheless has some of
the character of "false money," insofar as it is condemned to
remain in circulation.[35] The state can issue paper money at its
discretion, but it cannot subsequently withdraw it from circulation. And all the paper issued has to circulate; it is spent by the
recipients of public payments, who neither keep it nor hold it in
reserve. That is Marx's opinion. In contrast, H. Denis[36] and
Charles Rist[37] think that inconvertible fiat money can be put
away by private individuals and serve as a reserve of value,
even if only an imperfect and precarious one. In that sense
paper money would be a true but bad money; it would reproduce all the characteristics of the general monetary equivalent.
But Marx says nothing of the sort: on the contrary, he indicates
that gold cannot be replaced by things without value, by mere
symbols, except when it "is a mere coin, or means of circulation."[38] Paper money, true money insofar as it is a symbol of
gold, also partakes of the character of "false money" precisely
because it can never be anything but a symbol, condemned to
circulate without rest.

Only this last point, which is not made sufficiently specific and clear in *Capital*, could support the idea that Marx's monetary theory is mainly "metallicist" and that his criticism of the quantity theory therefore does not apply to paper money. And his agreement that immediate proportional changes in prices reestablish equilibrium shows to what extent Marx here remains under the influence of Ricardo. But the inadequacy of Marx's explanation on this point should not make us lose sight of the logic of his general concept of money, *completely opposed to that of the Quantity Theory of Money*. In this light, the fundamental problem posed by the circulation of fiat money with no intrinsic value is that of *the demonetization of all money in circulation by the very fact of its employment as an instrument of circulation*. The case of inconvertible fiat money is no different from that of coins; both involve the general problem of *reconciling the first two functions of money*.

The rate at which a token of value—whether it consists of paper or bogus gold and silver is quite irrelevant—can take the place of definite quantities of gold and silver calculated according to the mint-price depends on the number of tokens in circulation and by no means on the material of which they are made. The difficulty in grasping this relation is due to the fact that the two functions of money—as a standard of value and a medium of circulation—are governed not only by conflicting laws, but by laws which appear to be at variance with the antithetical features of the two functions. As regards its function as a standard of value, when money serves solely as money of account and gold merely as nominal gold, it is the physical material used which is the crucial factor. . . . On the other hand, when it functions as a medium of circulation, when money is not just imaginary but must be present as a real thing side by side with other commodities, its material is irrelevant and its quantity becomes the crucial factor.[39]

Thus in terms of the analysis of paper money one returns to the starting point of the general analysis of money as an instrument of circulation distinct from the measure of value on which it is based. It is necessary to recall briefly the difference between

the two functions, and its consequence; from it arises the need
for money's third function, as a means of hoarding.

The difference between the amount of commodity money with
a variable value originally produced, and the amount of money
with a given value in actual circulation, must be reabsorbed.
(Wicksell shows that he has not read *Capital* well when, to defend the quantity theory, he writes that Marx does not show
how this adjustment takes place or where the money goes that
is taken out of circulation.)[40] Nevertheless, by virtue of their very
difference, the two functions of money already analyzed are
both compatible with the possibility of a demonetization of the
money commodity. The measure of value does not imply the actual circulation of money, once there has been the initial exchange which makes it possible to set up the *equation of price*,
x commodity C=y money commodity. It is only money as instrument of circulation that makes it possible to establish the
formula for cash transactions, C-M-C (commodity-money-
commodity). But the money which circulates in causing commodities to circulate and is hence to be found present "side by
side with them" is not necessarily present as the money commodity. As currency, it can be represented by the symbol of
gold, and "Its functional existence absorbs, so to say, its material existence."[41] The differences of nature and quantity between
the measure of value and the currency both have the effect of
separating the general equivalent from its money form, the
specific commodity which functions as such in practice. From
this arises hoarding, the third function of money, which gold ful-
fills when "in person or by representative, it congeals into the
sole form of value, the only adequate form of existence of
exchange-value, in opposition to use-value, represented by all
other commodities."[42]

Money, Instrument of Hoarding

As the instrument of hoarding, money is "the money-commodity,
neither merely ideal, as in its function of a measure of value, nor
capable of being represented, as in its function of circulating
medium."[43] The paradox of this third function is that it introduces
money "proper" at the end of an analysis entirely devoted to

money. The place assigned to it, and the special role it plays as
the final element of a complete theory of money, should enable
us to understand why it is on the borderline between money and
credit, as well as between internal circulation and international
money.

1. Hoarding. Hoarding is an interruption in the circulation of commodities; the series of exchanges is broken and temporarily confined to the exchange C-M. This break reflects a desire to fasten M
down and keep it. "The money becomes petrified into a hoard, and
the seller becomes a hoarder of money."[44] Hoarding is a demand
for money as money, the general equivalent possessing special
qualities that distinguish it from all commodities.

Nevertheless money as an instrument of hoarding can only be
analyzed after the other two functions of money. It implies the
value of the money commodity, the basis of its commensurability
with all commodities. It likewise implies the actual circulation of
commodities; without this it would lose its own object, monetary
gold. Without the first two functions, the third would have no
meaning; it would be a simple demand for metal. Gold, thus
brought back from its "economic existence" to its "metallic existence," would disappear as money. But hoarding, in its turn,
plays a fundamental role in completing the economic definition
of money. Gold and silver "remain liquid as the crystallisation of
the process of circulation. But gold and silver establish themselves as money only in so far as they do not function as means
of circulation."[45]

Hoarding, the specific demand for money, serves to
ceaselessly preserve and reconstitute the money form as such,
whatever the deformations, transformations, and disappearances
it undergoes as a result of the other two functions. Produced by
these, it becomes in its turn a condition of their functioning. It
modifies the characteristics of each. Simultaneously, both the
"natural material" and the unit of account of the measure of
value (function No. 1) correspond to the "money form con-
gealed" by hoarding. On the other hand, "the withdrawal of
commodities from circulation in the form of gold is . . . the only
means of keeping them continuously in circulation"[46] and

guaranteeing the permanence of the second function of money by preserving the monetary character of the means of circulation. Thus hoarding helps to adjust the relationship between the measure of value and the medium of circulation. It absorbs the supply of money in excess of the needs arising from transactions. The original "supply" of the money commodity is balanced by a "demand" for money for transactions and a "demand" for "money as treasure," which serves as a fluctuating regulator.

"In order that the mass of money, actually current, may constantly saturate the absorbing power of the circulation, it is necessary that the quantity of gold and silver in a country be greater than the quantity required to function as coin. This condition is fulfilled by money taking the form of hoards. These reserves serve as conduits for the supply or withdrawal of money to or from the circulation, which in this way never overflows its banks."[47]

This regulatory function of hoarding can be fulfilled not only by gold but by every kind of currency.[48] It is one of the conditions of circulation; if it has a meaning, it is because money has a value and a specific form.

The role of hoarding, or the demand for money specifically as the "general equivalent," in unifying and regulating the functions of money, does not nevertheless abolish the contradictory characteristics inherent in monetary circulation. On the contrary, hoarding, which preserves the money form as distinct from all commodities, preserves at the same time the risks of disequilibrium involved in the circulation of commodities. To understand this it is necessary to consider the characteristics of its special dynamic.

The hoarder's desire for money "is in its very nature unsatiable."[49] It attaches itself to the "qualitative aspect" of money in which it "has no bounds to its efficacy . . . because it is directly convertible into any other commodity"[50]—what today is called the "liquidity" of money. But the amount of money that the hoarder can accumulate always remains limited, and hence relatively restricted in comparison with the infinite power of money. This results in a continual arbitrage between money in commerce and hoarded money.

One sees here what differentiates the hoarding analyzed by Marx from the liquidity preference defined by Keynes. Both imply a trade-off, between money and commodities according to Marx and between money and capital assets according to Keynes. This trade-off originates in the disequilibrium between a finite quantity (according to Marx) or a limited supply (according to Keynes) of disposable money and a specific quality of money, its universal power of exchange. Nevertheless, neither the conditions nor the effects of hoarding are the same in the two writers.

In a paradoxical way, it is Marx's analysis of hoarding which seems to be based entirely on the psychology of the hoarder: avarice, a taste for the esthetic qualities of gold, frenzied accumulation. . . . But these motives have a single object and a single effect which completely exhaust them as psychological causes. The greed of the hoarder is explained by the unique quality of money as general equivalent, and its function is to preserve the uniqueness. That is why it is "unsatiable." In contrast, Keynes's "liquidity preference," observable behavior in a monetary market and sensitive to variations in taxes and interest, is related to a "speculative motive" which is not completely determined by its function in the monetary market. There is a difference between the measurable tendency at the meeting point of the curves of demand for and supply of money and the cause which cannot be completely adequate to its own effects; this has given rise to innumerable discussions on the exact nature of cash hoarded for purposes of speculation and its difference from other forms of cash. In the background of the liquidity preference there is a zone of psychological shadow. Hence the differences between Marx's analysis and that of Keynes—which are connected with the fact that, for the moment, Marx is dealing with hoarding as it acts in simple circulation before capitalist markets evolve—are related to fundamental methodological and conceptual differences. Marx's seemingly more "psychological" description is entirely integrated into an analysis of the monetary role of hoarding, while Keynes's functional and psychological analysis leaves a psychological residue.

In attaching itself to the special quality of money as general equivalent, exchangeable for any commodity at all, hoarding nevertheless preserves, along with the normal functioning of money, the possibility of monetary disturbances which is already present in the other two functions of money. The circulation of commodities is interrupted, as well as preserved and regulated, by hoarding.

"Since the first metamorphosis of a commodity is at once a sale and a purchase, it is also an independent process in itself. The purchaser has the commodity, the seller has the money, i.e., a commodity ready to go into circulation at any time. No one can sell unless someone else purchases. But no one is forthwith bound to purchase, because he has just sold."[51]

This implies "the possibility, and no more than the possibility, of crisis."[52] For that reason the price form of the commodity can remain purely ideal, separate from any actual exchange. "Every trader knows that he is far from having turned his goods into money when he has expressed their value in a price or in imaginary money, and that it does not require the least bit of real gold to estimate in that metal millions of pounds' worth of goods."[53] If the money commodity's own value is the basis for the power of money as general equivalent, there is nevertheless no measure that can be applied to both that determinate value and the "infinite power" of money.

Hoarding thus completes the economic description of money in the simple circulation of commodities. One sees the unity of the functional aspects of money, as measure of value, instrument of circulation, and object of hoarding. One also sees how the separation of these functions disrupts the series of exchanges, so that monetary troubles represent the disequilibriums inherent in the circulation of commodities produced by private economic agents. The economic importance of money has to do not with the effect of variations in its quantity on prices, but with its form as general equivalent. Marx specifically says that simple circulation explains nothing, and that it has a "shallow and artificial character" because it depends "on circumstances all of which lie *outside* the framework of simple money circulation and are merely mirrored in it."[54] But this secondary character of money does not destroy its importance. At the end of his study, Marx has defined all the conditions of the economic existence of money. The money form only is preserved as such by virtue of the plurality of its functions and the insurmountable duality of its character, represented by the alternative hoarding-dishoarding.

This long analysis explains nothing, nothing except the conditions of the existence of money; by doing this, it prevents the disruptive intrusion of the analysis of money into that of production. Money is produced like other commodities, but it circulates in its own way. Behind all the simultaneous transactions, something is produced, an accumulation of money in the treasuries of individuals. The exchanges of all the equivalent products do not, therefore, necessarily take place at a given moment. The excess quantity of money of the quantitative analysts is only such in relation to a narrow concept of exchanges and a forced identification of commodities and money, followed by an equally forced contraposition of their quantities. Ricardo made the mistake of neglecting hoarding, through which money temporarily ceases to be a social flux and becomes the object of a private possession which restores it to its first state as general equivalent. Money does not just follow a straight course of demonetization and transformation into currency; it goes through a continuous circuit between non-circulation and circulation.

The result is that money, despite the secondary nature of its importance, is not *neutral* and can never be completely neutralized (whether by the development of credit or by monetary policy), since it puts into effect certain private decisions. Money in circulation really belongs to no one, but its very circulation is conditioned on the formation of hoards. These latter are reserves of value which sustain the value of the general equivalent. Their accumulation is sterile, for "Exclusion of money from circulation would also exclude absolutely its self-expansion as capital. . . ."[55] Marx follows Malthus in making a distinction between "saving" and "hoarding." But Ricardo is wrong in thinking that "to save is to spend," and to misinterpret hoarding as "accumulation of abstract wealth." Nevertheless this demand for value, fundamentally different from the demand for capital, gives an extra dimension to the world of transactions, forming a reservoir in it which can replace "saving" proper in the circulation of capital. The consequences of this theory of money will be analyzed in the second part of this study, following the plan of *Capital*. But from the first section on, Marx applies his concept in showing that every exchange of commodities implies a certain role of money.

2. Money as "Means of Payment" and "Universal Money." After the examination of hoarding, money "properly so-called" appears as "means of payment" and "universal money," i.e., as the means of settling transactions. "Gold becomes money, as distinct from coin, first by being withdrawn from circulation and hoarded, then by entering circulation as a non-means of circulation, finally however by breaking through the barriers of domestic circulation in order to function as universal equivalent in the world of commodities."[56] Only a very summary account is given here; the meaning of Marx's analyses must be found in the study of credit and the balance of payments.

Hoarding has appeared as a separation of the sale and purchase of commodities, or, to use Marx's customary symbols, C-M//. . .C. Money as means of payment plays its role at the end of a sale on credit, commodities having actually circulated without monetary means of circulation, in the pattern: C-credit. . .-M (means of payment). To settle with his creditor, the debtor has to sell C and put the money in reserve to pay on the due date. The whole chain of commercial credit can be put together from these transactions as a starting-point; they rest on the agreement of the parties to an exchange on their reciprocal obligations and rights. To meet the maturities, money enters into circulation as means of payment, it "appears to be the absolute commodity, but within the sphere of circulation, not outside it as with the hoards."[57] Nevertheless, in case of a commercial crisis, it is loudly hailed as the "unique form of wealth, exactly as it is regarded by the hoarder,"[58] and there is a "sudden transformation of the credit system into a monetary system."[59] This fundamental point, to be explained in the course of the analysis of credit, shows that the theory of money preserves its significance however much money may in practice be eliminated by credit.

Finally, the "universal money" is gold, the general equivalent, in "its original form of bullion."[60] "It is only in the markets of the world that money acquires to the full extent the character of the commodity whose bodily form is also the immediate social incarnation of human labour in the abstract. Its real mode of existence in this sphere adequately corresponds to its ideal concept."[61] All the functions of money are then fulfilled by this universal money. Nevertheless, "With the development of commodity exchange between different national spheres of circulation, the function which world money fulfils as *means of payment* for settling international balances develops also."[62]

Every country must establish a gold reserve fund. On this point, Marx accepts in part the validity of the mercantilist idea that states must establish gold stocks. In contrast, as will subsequently be seen, he completely rejects Ricardo's theory of the automatic equilibrium of the balance of payments.

Before developing these points, it is necessary to finish with the role attributed by Marx to money as such, as the object of hoarding, and as the instrument for the accumulation of reserves to settle credit and international transactions. In simple circulation it is possible to see some of the beginnings of the role of money in the financing of capitalist accumulation, when monetary reserves are set up for purposes of investment. But this new function, belonging to the capitalist economy, does not affect the validity of the theory of money, which takes account of all the economic effects attributable solely to "monetary relations" among economic entities.

There remains one last point to be considered here: if Marx's theory of money is general and complete, how does it incorporate the social and political effects of money with the economic effects?

d. Money and Social Power

According to the *Critique of Political Economy*, the acquisition of money is a source of power, primarily political. On the historical plane, Marx refers to it in the case of the absolute monarchy "which needs that material lever, the power of the *general equivalent*," convertible into any commodity and "always mobilizable"; this corresponds to the establishment of a general and uniform state power over the entire national territory.[63] In the same way a state, in its relations with other nations, needs a stock of gold, the universal money. "Behold the reason why, in the mercantilist system, gold and silver serve to measure the power of different societies." And Marx quotes Sir James Steuart: "As soon as the precious metals become objects of commerce, the universal equivalent for everything, they also become the measure of power between nations."[64]

This political effect of the possession of money explains the establishment of a hoard by the state. Nevertheless this public hoarding has the same roots as private hoarding. "Money is 'impersonal' property. It permits me to transport on my person, in my pocket, social power and social relations in general: the substance of society. Money puts social power in material form into the hands of private persons, who exercise it as individuals."[65]

But Marx did not retain these analyses of the political and social power inherent in money as a part of his theory of money. And the little that remains is found in a context that significantly modifies its meaning. Discussing the monetary role of the state, Marx has described how the state sets and guarantees the standard of coinage. He then writes: "Since the standard of money is on the one hand purely conventional, and must on the other hand find general acceptance, it is in the end regulated by law."[66]

Furthermore, the state mints the instrument of circulation and can itself issue monetary paper with compulsory currency, which has social validity by virtue of public coercive action.[67] That role permits it, for instance, to utilize the depreciation of the currency in relation to the gold which it supposedly represents by repaying its debts either in lighter money, without taking account of its effective devaluation, or in devalued money.[68] Because it is the guarantor of the nominal relationship between the monetary standard and the coinage, it can make use of the differences between the standardized weights of gold and coins in circulation. But that action takes place within the process of circulation; it does not imply any economic power of the state to determine the value of money. The monetary power of the state, which is genuine, is itself dependent on the "immanent laws" of monetary circulation, that is, on the determination of the money form in simple circulation in the way previously described. The social relation which is the basis for the existence and role of money is that of private exchange between private producers of commodities. It is a sign of an essential division of society, on which the economic power of money rests.

That is why the monetary power of the state is necessarily limited by the social power which money gives to the private individuals who hoard it. Public hoarding and private hoarding have the same root, but they are in opposition to one another. The state, or "the power which has become independent of society,"[69] hoards in order to consolidate its power over private individuals. But private hoarding means that "social power becomes the private power of private persons."[70] On the other hand, the public hoarding of a nation means that the monetary power of a state is limited by that of other states. The political and social effects of money are dependent on its economic nature as an expression of the division of society into autonomous economic individuals.

Thus one understands why Marx did not include in his theoretical exposition of the functions of money all the aspects of the power conferred by gold, but only those which are involved in the definition of money as a specific social relation. One can doubtless regret that Marx was not specific on this point; his analysis would have been more complete if he had given the reasons why it omitted certain elaborations. But one must not misinterpret these omissions, which are not lacunae, lest one fall into error subsequently in regard to the accumulation of money by capitalists and the role of banks and monetary policy.

TABLE OF THE FORMS OF MONEY

Functions	Formal Characters	Laws of Simple Circulation
		Origin of the general equivalent.
I. Measure of value. ↓ Standard of price.	Commodity of variable value, without price. Weights of gold with a conventionally fixed "monetary price."	Determination of the prices of commodities inversely proportional, all other things being equal to the value of money.
= money as "unit of account."		
II. Medium of circulation. ↓ currency: —minted coins. —inconvertible fiat money.	Value given, amount which circulates variable. Demonetization and gap between "monetary price" and "market price" of gold. Symbols of gold, although issued in arbitrary amount.	Factors of circulation: price, mass of commodities that circulate, speed of circulation of money (Possible effects on the numerical variations of commodity prices.)
I + II: Dematerialization of money		
III. Instrument of hoarding.	Demand for money "in person" as universal equivalent.	Absorption and preservation of the difference between the total money supply and money in circulation.
↓ Preservation of the form "general equivalent." →		Monetary base of capitalist credit, and international transactions.

PART TWO

MONEY
AND CAPITALISM

he basic purpose of *Capital* is the theoretical study of the capitalist form of production. If Marx began by constructing a theory of money valid for every monetary economy, it was because that same theory would be of service in the analysis of capitalism. Not only is it not subsequently called into question, but all the results obtained play their part in the totality of the exposition in *Capital*. Thus since money has already been defined as such, there is no subsequent monetary theory of capitalist phenomena. The theory of money bears solely on finance.

The integration of the theory of money into the theory of capitalist production is thus accomplished by the study of the modalities of capitalist financing. In a first stage, money appears as a capitalist instrument in its own right in such a way that the analysis of financing preserves the concept defined in the monetary analysis. The problem of financing is then only a financial problem, that of using the available money in proper amounts.

Nevertheless the specific mechanisms of finance which develop along with capitalist production form the "system of credit" which Marx distinguishes from the "monetary system." They must be studied as such. But if Marx, like Tooke and unlike Ricardo, makes a distinction between credit and money, it is because he adopts a monetary theory of credit and not a theory of credit money (similar to Schumpeter's distinction between *the monetary theory of credit* and *the credit theory of money*.)[1]

It is after resolving the general theoretical problem of money that Marx deals with all the specific financial problems of capitalism. His method rests on his theory of value, which is responsible for the order of problems and solutions and the combination of analyses of simple circulation, the circulation of capital, and the capital markets.

I. THE FINANCING OF CAPITALIST PRODUCTION

The financing problems connected with the "circulation of capital" analyzed in Part II involve the determination of the available monetary resources needed to permit productive capital to start functioning and to reproduce itself indefinitely. The financing of capitalist production is also the financing of the reproduction of capital (whether on the same scale, "simple reproduction," or on a different scale, "expanded reproduction.") That is why Marx begins by analyzing the concept of "money capital," describing the general conditions under which money plays a financial role in the circulation of capital.

The laws of simple circulation are first brought into question by the production of surplus value, which disrupts the exchange of equivalent commodities. The capitalist, who purchases the means of production and labor power for a value $M = C$, profits at the end of the productive process by a surplus value m and finds himself in the possession of a sum of money $M' = M + m$, larger than his initial expenses.[2] But the laws of the circulation of capital are subject to those of simple circulation, insofar as the reproduction of capital implies a definite amount of money not only at the beginning of the process but at its end, which is itself necessarily the beginning of a new process of circulation of capital.

The role of money capital depends not only on this movement of capital, but on the patterns of reproduction of the social product M' and their state of equilibrium during a given period. The proportions necessary if money as such is to play its role as a capitalist instrument are defined in successive stages, first in the functioning of the capital cycle M-C. .P. .C'-M', then in the social product cycle C'. . .M-C. .P. .C'.

A. MONEY AND THE CAPITAL CYCLE

In the first part of Volume II, Marx sums up the whole process of the circulation of capital as follows:[3]

I. M-C. . .P. . .C'-M'   money-capital cycle
II. P. . .Tc. . .P   productive capital cycle
III. Tc. . .P(C')   commodity-capital cycle

The meaning of the symbols used has already been indicated, except for P, production, and Tc, the total process of circulation. The first cycle, that of money capital, represents "the movement of capital" common to the three cycles, i.e., "the valorization of value" M. . .M'. At the beginning of the whole process is money capital or "capital in monetary form" as the "prime motor" for every capitalist who starts a business and has to buy productive commodities (labor power, means of production.) Just as the circulation of commodities presupposes the circulation of money, so the circulation of capital implies that of money capital. This is present not only at the beginning of the cycle, but also at its end, where capital reappears in the monetary form M'. Money capital constantly accompanies the productive and reproductive movement of industrial capital. As the means of financing, it shows the effect of the general laws of simple circulation, and of the existence of money, on capitalist production. "We see . . . money in general is the form in which every individual capital (apart from credit) must make its appearance in order to transform itself into productive capital; this follows from the nature of capitalist production and of commodity production in general."[4]

But this role of money does not pose any new monetary problem; there is only a problem of financial proportions, that of adjusting the quantity of money capital to the requirements of the production and reproduction of capital. Before developing this point, it is useful to group the symbols M-C. . .P. . .C'-M'· in the following table:

Investments of Capitalists	Production	Resources of Capitalists

Monetary   Real
 	
M = C
	C. . .P. . .C'
	
	• Labor power
	  producing
	  surplus value "c"
	• Means of
	  production
		Real Monetary
		
		C' = C + c = M + m = M'

Money M, used for the purchase of commodities for production, is "advanced" by the capitalist at the beginning of the first cycle of the process because "Capital in the form of money must always be available for the payment of wages, before production can be carried on capitalistically."[5] The "productive" investments of the capitalist are represented by M-C. If money can buy labor power, it is because this is a function of money as medium of circulation, which the capitalist spends as *money* capital. There is really an exchange of equivalents between the advances of money on the one side and wages and means of production on the other. But if money can be spent for wages and can put labor power at the disposal of the capitalist, it is because it serves here as money *capital*. The relation between buyer and seller becomes the relation between capitalist and wage-laborer, which alone "permits of the transformation of a mere money-function into a capital-function."[6] *Money capital* thus represents a specific relation between social relationships of different types. "In the relation of capitalist and wage-labourer, the relation between the buyer and the seller, the money-relation, a relation inherent in production."[7]

Undoubtedly the form of production takes precedence over the form of exchange, and that of capital over that of money. But the monetary relation "immanent" in the capitalist relation preserves its nature and its specific role. Capital *must* return to a monetary form for the initial exchange M-C to be able to take place and reproduce itself.

It is of little importance here what kind of money is used: metal money, credit money, token money, etc. The sole fundamental monetary requirement is "that the capital to be advanced must be advanced in the form of money."[8] But the *amount* advanced should be adequate, because "The process of circulation of industrial capital . . . is determined by the general laws previously set forth (Volume I, Chapter III), in so far as it is only a series of acts within the general circulation of commodities."[9]

If the quantity C is given by hypothesis, the amount of money advanced depends, all other things being equal, on the rapidity of monetary circulation or, if the rapidity is given, on the cost of the commodities, or if the rapidity and cost are given, on the value of the money itself. If the quantity C is taken as a variable, the amount of M varies as a function of C: "that portion of the advanced capital-value which must be continually advanced and renewed in the form of money differs in its ratio to the productive capital which it sets in motion, i.e., in its ratio to the continuous scale of production, depending on the particular length of the period of turnover[10] and the particular ratio between its two component parts—the working period and the period of circulation."[11]

The amount M is then a function of the requirements of the production to be financed. Nevertheless, whatever the origin of the variations of M as a function of C and the amount of M required in relation to the quantity C, "the portion of the capital-value in process which can continually function as productive capital is limited in any event by that portion of the advanced capital-value which must always exist beside the productive capital in the form of money."[12]

What does that *limit* represent, if not the effect of monetary financing on the movement of productive capital? Undoubtedly the *scale* and *efficiency* of capitalist production are not dependent on financial resources, which in no way constitute the "absolute limits" of the process of production. The results of the use of the productive commodities C, financed by M, are not and cannot be directly proportional to the volume of money capital advanced, since they depend on the effectiveness of the concrete elements which in combination constitute *productive capital*. This difference between the effects of financial resources in their own right and the effects attributable to their productive use gives the formal difference between money capital and productive capital a content such that capital undergoes real metamorphoses in the course of its circulation. Hence the "limit" fixed by the amount M available at the beginning of the process is *relative* to the whole process of circulation, as is shown by the existence at the end of the process of M', or M + m. And this *"relative"* limit set by financial resources means simply that the concept of money capital is a relation between two distinct terms which cannot be merged.

One cannot derive the function of money from its character of capital, nor that of capital from its money form, according to Marx;[13] to do so is to misunderstand both money and capitalism.

The problem of financing thus reduces itself to the determination of the suitable proportions of M in relation to C. In the case of *simple reproduction*, the maintenance of the same scale of production, the final difference between M and M' (the surplus value in its monetary form *m*) is entirely spent by the capitalist on consumption goods. The capitalist spends all the surplus value as revenue (no hoarding) but not more (no dishoarding for consumption). Without this last condition, the amount M advanced at the beginning of the cycle would not function entirely as money capital; there would be "disinvestment" and a break in the circuit of capital. Money would lose its character of capital and capital would cease to reproduce itself through its various metamorphoses. Simple reproduction implies the preservation of M as means of financing. The capitalist cannot then consume more than $c = m$. The expenditure of m on objects of consumption, a real "flight" out of the circuit of reproduction, absorbs c, the surplus of commodities produced; its role is then entirely defined by its function *within* the circuit of simple reproduction.

In the same way the commodities c consumed by the capitalist are here simply non-productive commodities, corresponding to money not invested. Marx has not yet analyzed the composition of the social product and distinguished objects of consumption from the means of production "from the point of view of the replacement of the value as well as the substance of the individual component parts of C'."[14] In terms of the financing of simple reproduction described so far, the consumption of c has meaning only in relation to the preservation of the ratios M-C. . .C'-M'. The problem of financing is resolved *before* the problem of division of the social product is posed. At this stage of Marx's argument the problem of financing is not even really a financial problem, in the sense that *by hypothesis* the capitalist has money at the beginning of the process of the circulation of capital and can spend it for productive commodities, i.e., invest it, recover it, reinvest it, etc.

This hypothesis explains why Marx speaks of simple reproduction and the consumption of surplus value by the capitalist *before* completely analyzing the social product. Here the consumption of c is in terms of the closing of the circuit M...M'...M. This is also why Marx speaks without distinction of simple reproduction by the capitalist or by the capitalist class. "What is true of the individual capitalist, applies to the capitalist class."[15]

The circuit closes itself in the same way whether the capitalist consumes all his surplus value or all the capitalists consume all the surplus value produced. The interdependent decisions bearing on consumption, investment, and financing, still have no content other than that of the exchange of equivalent commodities: c, the surplus of commodities, is necessarily sold (bought) in exchange for m. This exchange of equivalents has as its only object and effect the preservation of the circuit of capital, "individual" *or* total, "individual" *and* total, disregarding for the moment the socially complementary nature of the various commodities produced and the various economic agents.

The analysis of the financing of *reproduction on an enlarged scale* adds nothing essentially new to that of simple reproduction; it nevertheless permits the clarification of the specific effect of the money form of capital.

Instead of consuming the entire surplus value, the capitalist can put part or all of it aside to invest and produce on an enlarged scale. He "saves," i.e., he does not spend as revenue the whole surplus value created by his workers, but he does not "hoard" if the profit is immediately spent on additional productive commodities. The financing of reproduction on an enlarged scale rests on the "abstinence" of the "capitalist of the classical type" which Marx has already mentioned in Volume I, particularly in reference to Malthus.[16]

Nevertheless accumulation can require a certain hoarding of surplus value "until it has increased sufficiently for the extension of his old business or the opening of a side-line."[17] Everything depends on the degree to which the process of production can be expanded at a given moment in the different branches of industry. Deferred investment implies the establishment of a reserve fund and hence "hoarding." This is provisional and relative; it represents "a part of capital in a preliminary stage of its accumulation" and "latent money capital."[18] But it still comes under the general definition of hoarding as the interruption of the series of exchanges. "So long as the formation of the hoard continues, it does not increase the demand of the capitalist. The money is immobilized. It does not withdraw from the commodity-market any equivalent in commodities for the money-equivalent withdrawn from it for commodities supplied.[19] "The formation of a hoard thus appears here as a factor included in the process of capitalist accumulation, accompanying it, but nevertheless essentially different from it; for the process of reproduction is not expanded by the formation of latent capital. On the contrary, latent money-capital is here formed because the capitalist producer cannot at once expand the scale of his production."[20]

The effect of the process thus described by Marx would today be called "deflationary" disequilibrium. The limits of the financing of individual enterprises can unquestionably be pushed back by the centralization of the capitals of a section of the capitalists, and by means of credit;[21] the redistribution of available resources for the profit of the investors is a means of more rapidly and efficiently solving the problem of the mobilization of the necessary funds. But this does not remove the necessity for social saving in monetary form, without which there would be danger of troubles, this time "inflationary."[22]

Thus in capitalist production, hoarding preserves the ambivalence that it has in simple circulation. As an interruption of the process of circulation, it plays a role which is at the same time destructive of equilibrium and regulative. The preservation of that duality shows that money as an instrument of capitalism preserves its own monetary functions. Thus Marx, having constructed his general theory of money before examining the role of money in capitalism, finds his method vindicated.

B. MONEY AND REPRODUCTION OF THE SOCIAL PRODUCT

There is no specific problem, either monetary or even financial, in regard to the circulation of capital in the form M-

C. . .P. . .C'-M'. *By hypothesis* the sum of money M is at the disposal of the capitalist at the beginning of the cycle of money-capital and is again present at the beginning of the circuit once the first one has been completed. Nor does the money used as money-capital *while preserving its own functions* present any new monetary problem; the conditions of equilibrium of simple circulation are again found in the attributes of the circulation of capital.

It is nevertheless not possible to stop there, since the complementary character of the decisions on saving and investment by the agents of the financing has not yet been considered. It is by virtue of the restrictive hypotheses referred to above that Marx was able, as a first stage, to analyze capitalist financing before examining all the conditions of the reproduction of the social product. The theoretical results obtained in this first stage remain valid in the rest of the analysis. They are indispensable to understand the terms and solutions of the problem of financing in a second stage, and this in turn must be traversed for a complete determination of the conditions of financing.

At the end of the first stage, the circulation of money already appears "as an immanent element of the process of reproduction" of capital. But that "immanence" is only completely intelligible after the analysis of the patterns of simple and expanded reproduction of the social product, which shows the need for a financial equilibrium between the balance-sheets of the capitalists producing different commodities.

Marx, in fact, introduces a new method of analyzing the "circulation of capital." He divides social production into two main sections, the production of the means of production (Department I) and the production of the means of consumption (Department II). He breaks down the value of the product of each of these departments into constant capital consumed within the year, variable capital (wages), and surplus value. Letting c_1 and c_2 represent the constant capital included in the product of the two departments, v_1 and v_2 the variable capital, and s_1 and s_2 the surplus value, the value of the total product equals $c_1 + c_2 + v_1 + v_2 + s_1 + s_2$. Marx analyzes the reproduction of the social product by studying the relations among these components. Equality between the sum of the variable capital (wages) and the surplus value included in the product of Department I and the constant capital expended by the capitalists of Department II, expressed by the equation $v_1 + s_1 + c_2$, is the condition for general equilibrium of the balance-sheets of all capitalists. This equilibrium Marx studies from a financial point of view "in its primitive form."[23] i.e., in terms of a monetary circulation carried out in metallic form, with no intervention of credit operations. Consequently the capitalists producing gold play a role that has to be integrated into the whole pattern. It follows that the financing of investments rests here on the "self-financing" of the capitalists.

These last points show how far Marx remains faithful to his initial method in regard to the analysis of money. *Even in analyzing the pattern of the reproduction of the social product*, although it represents a different level of analysis, he is able to use *the results obtained in the examination of simple circulation in general and the circulation of capital* in the form M-C. . .P. . . C′-M′. But in order to avoid errors in interpretation, it is necessary to understand *how* Marx proceeds. Here again there is great disorder in the exposition, and Marx's plan often seems confused. It is important to reconstruct carefully the *articulation* of the two stages of the financial analysis of the circulation of capital, before going on to examine financing *within* the pattern of reproduction as a whole.

a. The Circulation of Surplus Value
One asks oneself why, at the end of the analysis of the circulation of capital within the framework M-C. . .P. . .C′-M′, Marx discusses what he calls the question of the "circulation of surplus value," a question he poses as follows:

An opponent of Tooke, who clings to the formula M-C-M′, asks him how the capitalist manages always to withdraw more money from circulation than he throws into it. Mind you! The question at issue here is not the formation *of surplus-value. This, the only secret, is a matter of course from the capitalist standpoint. The sum of values employed would not be capital if it did not enrich itself by means of surplus-value. But as it is capital by assumption, surplus-value is taken for granted.*

The question, then, is not where the surplus-value comes from but whence the money comes into which it is turned.[24]

Marx answers: the problem of the circulation of surplus value does not exist, but this false problem . . . has a true solution. This means that in terms of the analyses already made, no new monetary or financial problem presents itself, and that the only additional clarifications called for at the moment are of a technical nature.

1. The problem of financing surplus value does not exist as a monetary or financial problem. In fact, if one asks where the money comes from to "monetize surplus value," one must ask where the money comes from to finance the purchase of C at the beginning of the cycle M-C. In thus generalizing the problem, one abolishes it. Or is it a question of finding the amount of money needed to finance production, and then: "So far as any problem exists here, it coincides with the general problem: Where does the money required for the circulation of the commodities of a certain country come from?"[25]

The general solution has already been given by the laws of simple circulation, in the theory of money.

Or the question is that of the initial appropriation of a supply of money by the capitalists. But this is included in the question, analyzed elsewhere,[26] of the historical conditions for the creation of a capitalist class. Here it is assumed that the capitalist is the "money-man," the man who can lay out the money to buy commodities for production and for consumption as well. "But it is a decided trait of the capitalist to be able to live on means in his possession until surplus-value begins to return."[27]

In any case, there is no special problem of "the circulation of surplus-value," and Marx is quite right to say: *the problem itself therefore does not exist*,"[28] the more so as he has limited it to a problem of "circulation" and not of "realization" of surplus value. Has he thus juggled away the second problem in favor of the first, and made the question of the "real demand" purely one of monetary availability? Rosa Luxemburg thought so, asking in vain where the demand for accumulated surplus value was to be found in the system of reproduction. This would have meant that Marx overestimated the financial aspect of the accumulation of capital at the expense of its "real" aspect. We will return to this point subsequently, after examining the whole analysis of financing.[29]

2. Some technical clarifications are nevertheless necessary in regard to the way a supply of gold is obtained. Marx here introduces the capitalists who produce gold, incorporating their role into the format M-C. . .P. . .C'-M' in the following way:

Appropriated by the Capitalists	(Production)	Resources of the Capitalists
M = C	Gold Commodities	Other capitalists
Gold producers		$c = m$
$m = c$		C' = M'

This diagram indicates that the producers of gold can *immediately* spend the commodity they produce. "The product is money even in its bodily form; there is no need therefore of transforming it into money by means of exchange, by a process of circulation. . . . The money-form of the circulating capital consumed in labor-power and means of production is replaced, not by the sale of the product, but by the bodily form of the product itself; hence, not by once more withdrawing its value from circulation in money-form, but by additional, newly produced money."[30]

Hence, whereas one part of the capitalist class throws into circulation commodities greater in value, (greater by the amount of surplus-value) than the money-capital advanced by them, another part of the capitalists throws into circulation money of greater value (greater by the amount of the surplus-value) than the com-

modities which they constantly withdraw from circulation for the production of gold. Whereas one part of the capitalist class constantly pumps more gold out of the circulation than it pours into it, the part that produces gold constantly pumps more money into it than it takes out in means of production.[31]

The process thus described follows from the preceding analyses (no "hoarding" by the producers of gold, etc.). It simply represents the technical solution of the general problem of monetary circulation which has already been solved on the theoretical plane.

These are the two aspects of Marx's response to the false problem of the circulation of surplus value. But the second point obviously has a transitory and even transitional character. The technical response to the general problem of monetary circulation, if it is not a mere tautology (the function of the producers of gold being . . . to produce gold), implies the insertion of the role of these producers *within* the system of circulation, as has been done above. But there is a danger that this diagram itself will lead to confusion. For it indicates that to get gold the capitalists sell all their surplus value to the producers of gold, so that their surplus value "m" is equal to the total surplus value, and the entire surplus product of society therefore passes through their hands.[32] That would make no sense in terms of the system of reproduction (C′. . .C′). *Valid for the first stage of the analysis* of circulation, *the diagram becomes absurd in the second stage,* that of the equilibrium of the balance-sheets of all capitalists producing different commodities (including the producers of gold). That is why it has a transitional significance. The production of gold, *the technical solution of a monetary problem long since solved,* is also *the indication of a new financial problem which has not yet been posed. Here is the connection between the two major parts of the monetary analysis of financing.* The intrinsic linkage between the financial and "real" mechanisms of accumulation is only obtained insofar as the capacity of the capitalists for financing is integrated into the whole set of conditions under which the social product is reproduced.

In the second stage of the analysis of financing it is necessary first to integrate the balance-sheet of the producers of gold into the totality of balance-sheets in conformity with the conditions for equilibrium, and then clarify the financial requirements of general equilibrium for all capitalists.

b. The Financial Requirements for Equilibrium

1. The relations between the balance-sheets of the producers of gold, as capitalists of Department I, and those of capitalists of Department II, must be subject to the condition of equilibrium $v_1 + s_1 = c_2$. But at first one does not see how this is possible since the producers of gold only sell a small portion of their product as constant industrial capital cm.

Marx gives some examples in figures, which appear in the following table:

DEPARTMENT I SUB-SECTION OF PRODUCERS OF GOLD		DEPARTMENT II CAPITALISTS PRODUCING COMMODITIES FOR CONSUMPTION	
Appropriations	Resources	Appropriations	Resources
$5v_1$	$2\,c_2$ industrial gold	$2\,c_2$ industrial gold	$5\,v_1$
$5s_1$	$8\,c_2$ gold money	$8\,c_2$ hoarded gold	$5\,s_1$
Total 10	10	10	10

The major part of the appropriations $v1 + s1$ is compensated by the monetary resources of the producers of gold, which correspond to hoarding by the capitalists of Department II. Equilibrium is obtained in terms of the equation "money produced = hoarding." Without this the producers of gold would have a deficit, and the capitalists of Department II would not be able to invest in c_2 the resources derived from the sale of their products for an amount $v_1 + s_1$. Hoarding here has the character of an appropriation in constant capital.

Two complementary points should be noted: *the status of the producers of gold as part of Department I* on the one hand, and on the other, the meaning in respect to *hoarding by the capitalists of Department II*. According to Marx, "The production of gold, like that of metals generally, belongs to Department I, the category which embraces the production of means of production."[33]

In her work *The Accumulation of Capital* Rosa Luxemburg criticizes this concept of Marx, and proposes to distinguish a *third department*, that of, the production of the means of exchange. She argues that money, useless for both consumption and industrial production, is produced as a specific commodity and should be included in a special section of the social product.

In saying this, Rosa Luxemburg appears completely faithful to Marx's theory of money, more faithful than Marx himself! For a third department, that of the production of the medium of circulation, would have as its product money as such, an indispensable instrument of capitalist reproduction but a medium of circulation relatively independent of and much older than capitalism.[34] Money would thus be incorporated into the system of capitalist reproduction in a way appropriate to its own nature as the specific incarnation of "abstract social labor"[35] in all commodity production.

Nevertheless, I think that this involves an error of interpretation which undermines Marx's theory of money. For the creation of a third department, devoted to the production of means of circulation, gives money the character of a *third kind of commodity* and thus of a commodity *on the same plane* as the others. To isolate the production of gold in order to respect the special character of money is in fact to destroy that special character, which contraposes money to all commodities. When Marx includes the production of gold in Department I, it is because the monetary character of gold as "general equivalent" does not result from the particular character of its production as a commodity.[36]

This error by Rosa Luxemburg is coupled with an incorrect interpretation of the role of the hoarding of the gold produced, the second point to be noted here. Indeed, Rosa Luxemburg thinks that, since money cannot serve as productive capital, the insertion of the production of gold into Department I implies a social deficit in the means of production equal to the gold produced, or 8 for the capitalists of Department II in terms of the figures used above. The condition of equilibrium, $r_1 + s_1 = c_2$, is no longer satisfied, since the capitalists of Department II cannot use gold as a means of production c_2. Since the production of gold cannot be usefully absorbed by the capitalists producing consumption goods, its insertion into Department I upsets the equilibrium of the system of reproduction.

It is true that hoarding is by definition a non-demand for commodities and that the capitalist producer of consumption goods, who does not need the newly produced gold to buy the means of production or pay wages, and cannot spend additional gold for his own consumption, is forced to hoard. But Rosa Luxemburg is in error in not making clear the special function of hoarding here. According to Marx, the hoarded gold is a fraction of the constant capital of Department II, and therefore, "even simple reproduction . . . necessarily includes the storing up, or hoarding, of money. And as this is annually repeated, it explains the assumption from which we started in the analysis of capitalist production, namely, that at the beginning of the reproduction a supply of money corresponding to the exchange of commodities is in the hands of the capitalists of Departments I and II."[37]

From this point of view, hoarding has the meaning of an "investment" in money, by which the supply of money needed for transactions is formed and re-formed. This investment in gold is a special form of hoarding which, Marx says, parallels the annual production of gold. Far from upsetting the general equilibrium of production, this hoarding guarantees its continuance, on the secondary level where it produces its effect.

In all cases, hoarding has the same general definition as an interruption of the series of exchanges. But its effect is modified in terms of its function in the systems of reproduction. Marx differentiates the hoarding which absorbs the new production of gold from that which corresponds to the amortization of capital and the net investment, and which is an element of the general financial equilibrium of the balance-sheets of the capitalists.[38]

2. Given the value of money and the necessary and sufficient amount of gold, the problem of financing which Marx goes on to discuss is that of adjusting the decisions of the capitalists who save in monetary form, i.e., hoard, and those of the capitalists who dishoard when they invest. (This concerns only a special aspect of gross saving and investment, which are necessarily equal *ex post facto*.)[39]

The complementary effects of these decisions at a given moment can guarantee financial equilibrium if it is at the same time otherwise in accordance with the laws of monetary circulation, those of the circulation of capital, and the specific requirements of the reproduction of the social product.

One could, Marx says, imagine the possibility of simultaneous hoarding by all the capitalists (except the producers of gold). He immediately[40] adds that in terms of the systems of reproduction, this hypothesis is absurd. But it permits a genuine argument from the absurd, whose conclusion is that "accumulation in the form of money never takes place simultaneously at all points."[41] That is, the decisions on hoarding and dishoarding balance one another at a given moment. Marx shows this in regard to simple reproduction[42] in discussing the financing of accumulation in Department I:

It is evident that both the investments of capital in the numerous lines of industry constituting Department I, and the different individual investments of capital within each of these lines of industry, according to their age, i.e., the space of time during which they have already functioned, quite aside from their volumes, technical conditions, market conditions, etc., are in different stages of the process of successive transformation from surplus-value into potential money-capital. . . . One part of the capitalists is continually converting its potential money-capital, grown to an appropriate size, into productive capital. Another part of the capitalists is meanwhile still engaged in hoarding its potential money-capital. Capitalists belonging to these two categories confront each other: some as buyers, the others as sellers, and each one of the two exclusively in one of these roles.[43]

The same analysis applies to accumulation in Department II.[44]

The decisions of the one group in regard to expenditures for investment and of the other in regard to hoarding should therefore balance one another at a given moment. Indeed, the question has to do strictly with the financial conditions of reproduction. For the condition of general equilibrium, the equation $v_1 + s_1 = c_2$, implies in contrast the *simultaneous* sale and purchase of the various commodities making up the social product, i.e., the *absence* of hoarding. It also involves the distinction between the annual *"saving"* and hoarding. For all the product of Department I to be sold, it must be absorbed by the demand of the capitalists of the two departments for the means of production. (This corresponds to a "gross annual saving.")[45] But the fact remains that during the same period a part of the capitalists hoard, and thus sell without buying. The effect of this hoarding must be counterbalanced by the demand of the other capitalists who spend their monetary reserves. The "pure supply" of commodities of the one group must be counterbalanced by the "pure demand" of the other, or reciprocally the hoarding of one part of the capitalists must be neutralized by a "pure supply" of money.[46] The reserves previously set up for amortization of fixed capital and net investment cannot be simultaneously expended by all the enterprises; at the same time as some capitalists hoard, others must put their monetary reserves into circulation in the market for means of production, in such a way that the global equilibrium of gross investment and "saving" may be guaranteed without financial disturbances.

Nevertheless the counterbalancing of hoarding and dishoarding necessarily involves an element of uncertainty. Undoubtedly the financial decisions are here subordinated to the conditions of reproduction as a whole, and do not operate autonomously. The impossibility of simultaneous hoarding by all capitalists is one of the conditions for the possibility of the reproduction of the social product. But Marx analyzes *capitalist* reproduction, the conditions for whose equilibrium are ultimately the result of the contradictory effects of private decisions. And the *complementary* relation between the balance-sheets of different capitalists, which is on the financial plane simultaneously a consequence and a condition of the system of reproduction, is only actualized by a *compensation after the fact*, which includes the risk of financial disorder. Money, now completely defined as an "immanent element of the process of reproduction," retains its ambivalent effect along with its specific character. Its "immanence" is never, according to Marx, its "neutrality."

Everything is in accord with the principles of Marx's monetary theory, based on the law of value and the significance of the general equivalent. The conditions of the balanced financing of capitalist reproduction include money as a specific social relationship between *private* producers. Marx's financial analysis thus differs not only from that of J. B. Say, for example, but from the theories of monetary equilibrium which follow Walras; according to these latter, the excess demand for money is zero only when monetary equilibrium is present simultaneously with equilibrium in the market for goods (that is when $M^d - M^s = O$ while $G^s - G^d = 0$). Money is neutral when there is general equilibrium. Undoubtedly part of Marx's analysis, which I am about to describe, seems to fit this concept of equilibrium, since the excess demand for money must be compensated for by an equivalent demand for commodities. But the concepts actually differ fundamentally. For Marx money is not neutral, even in equilibrium, since its financial role is included in the system of capitalist reproduction, where the combination of decisions is the *subsequent* effect of relations of interdependence. Hence the nature and significance of money as general equivalent are preserved, whether there is financial equilibrium or disequilibrium. Equilibrium *and* disequilibrium between hoarding and dishoarding both show the continued presence of money as a specific social relation. Thus money is not "neutral" even when "neutralized" in equilibrium.

This is a further reason why it seems to me impossible to conceive of the production of money as belonging to a third department of the social product. The Marxist economist Paul M. Sweezy, for theoretical reasons different from those of Rosa Luxemburg, thinks it necessary to set money apart, this time produced as a "unit of account" whose value would be identical with its price.[47] Sweezy does not first reconstitute Marx's theory of money; he only gets to money when explaining the systems of reproduction. According to Marx, these systems should show how the commodities produced can be exchanged in the required proportions, in accordance with their values, *with the value of money given*. The determination of prices does not come in here, whether because it has already been explained in the theory of money or because it involves other conditions which will only be explained later, in examining the formation of the average rate of profit. Sweezy, on the other hand, follows Bortkiewicz in trying to interpret the systems of reproduction with reference to the prices of commodities. He formulates the equations of reproduction in terms of relative prices and introduces a supplementary equation, that of the unit of account. The monetary prices of commodities are calculated in units of the money commodity, produced by a certain number of hours of labor and with a price assumed to be equal to its value. This hypothesis permits the preservation on an overall basis of the equality between the sum of the prices and the sum of the values of all commodities. It implies that the production of gold takes place under conditions such that the organic composition of the capital of section III (that is, the relation between the expenditures of constant and variable capital, the relation between c and v) is equal to the average social organic composition, or in other words that the production of money takes place under neutral capitalist conditions. But this is not Marx at all, but rather Ricardo, who sought as an invariable standard of prices a commodity produced under the average conditions of social production, and who accepted the hypothesis that gold could play that role. Money thus conceived in terms of specific type of production would be defined as money by the circumstances of its production.

In proceeding thus, Sweezy calls into question Marx's theory of money and the financial conditions of reproduction by upsetting the order of the reasoning. He introduces the problem of the prices of commodities into the systems of reproduction, where Marx has excluded this problem by hypothesis and taken the value of money and the value of commodities as givens. If money is treated as a unit of account possessing a price, it loses its specificity, and if its price is equal to its labor value, it can be considered as neutral. The confusion of the problem of prices and that of the conditions of reproduction, and the introduction of a money-commodity unit of account, wreck the bases of Marx's theory of money.

In contrast, the whole examination of financing described here shows that money as a financial instrument preserves its specific characteristics as a non-commodity, and that there is consequently no *monetary problem* of financing on the theoretical plane. Financial equilibrium of the balance-sheets of the industrial capitalists requires only that the combination of the monetary social relationship and the capitalist social relationship observe the prescribed proportions. But this combination does not detract from the role of the monetary relationship when it has become "immanent" in capitalist reproduction. In simple circulation, money as general equivalent is distinct from all the commodities exchanged by private producers. In the circulation of capital "money-capital evidently plays a prominent role, seeing that it is the form in which the variable capital is advanced,"[48] insofar as "the wage system predominates."[49] The use of the money is thus doubly determined by the social relationships between private economic agents. But money still remains true to its nature, witness the financial role of hoarding.

At the end of this analysis of the financing of capitalist reproduction one sees how Marx conceived the joint role of money and capital in the circulation of capital M-C. . .P. . .C'-M' and in the reproduction of the social product C'. . .C'. This approach has been subjected to different but converging criticisms. According to some, including Rosa Luxemburg, Marx attached too much importance to the capacity of the capitalists for investment, neglecting the real conditions for the stimulation of investment. Moreover the analysis of financing gives money a functional role, since hoarding is subordinated to the will of the capitalists to invest. The theory of accumulation, simultaneously too monetary and insufficiently so, leads to a static conception, that of the general equilibrium of exchanges, rather than to a knowledge of the actual conditions of investment.

It is true that the accumulation of capital, reduced to its abstract mechanism, merges its own real and financial conditions; the stimulus to invest is then only an aspect of the capacity to invest, which implies a determinate division of the social product. *Neither long term nor cyclical problems come in at this stage of the analysis;* when they do come under consideration, it is in connection with other analyses, especially those relating to cyclical financial disequilibrium. Above all, Marx does not give a monetary theory of accumulation which would collapse under a double criticism of underestimating or overestimating the role of money. The question is that of *the financing of accumulation in a monetary economy,* where the circulation of money is combined with that of capital. Since the theory of money is not mixed up with that of production, there is no monetary theory of the "realization of surplus value" or of the accumulation of capital.

The specifically monetary analysis of financing takes place in the discussion of credit, which introduces new elements. The problem of the financial equilibrium of balance-sheets, so far confined to its "natural and primitive form" (on the basis of metallic money and self-financing) and its general functional aspect (without taking cyclical metamorphoses into consideration), will become much more complex. But the discussion which follows involves the knowledge and use of all the monetary and financial concepts analyzed up to this point.

II. CREDIT: STRUCTURES AND CYCLE

Some introductory remarks are necessary here. My explanation of the theory of money and of the financing of capitalist reproduction has adhered to the order of argument indicated by Marx himself, whatever the confusion of certain passages of *Capital.* The analysis of credit should be conducted in the same way to reconstitute the *monetary theory of credit* logically. The coherence of Marx's theory of money is evidence of the cohesion of *Capital* on the basis of the scientific abstraction developed by Marx.

But a careful reading of *Capital* shows a seemingly insurmountable obstacle: the texts in regard to credit were scarcely edited by Marx. In his preface to Volume III (dated October 4, 1894), Engels points out the difficulties of editing the last part of *Capital*: "The greatest difficulty was presented by Part V, which treated of the most complicated subject in the entire volume"—credit! "Here, then," says Engels, "we had no finished draft, not even a scheme whose outlines might have been filled out, but only the beginning of an elaboration—often just a disorderly mass of notes, comments and extracts."[50]

This is particularly true of the chapters dealing with the machinery of banking, polemics on credit policy, and the balance of payments. Does it make sense under these conditions, even with the arrangement of the material by Engels, to confer the name of "Theory of credit" on the notes accumulated by Marx, and to present their theoretical content? Does one have the right to "write" *Capital* on this point while pretending to "read" it?

The difficulty is nevertheless not insurmountable for several reasons. First, if Marx did not edit all his notes on credit, at least he wrote them, and their great number shows the extent of his theoretical, historical, and political knowledge of the field. But above all, in the course of his previous discussions, *Marx assigned a definite place to the analysis of credit*. Since the financial mechanisms in question were not a simple expression of the monetary mechanisms already considered, they could not be studied before or simultaneously with them. The logical order which makes it possible *to give the part of Volume III dealing with credit its proper place within* Capital, likewise makes it possible to dissect it in a logical way, by methods similar to those used thus far. One can thus illuminate an essential point, the logical relation between the theory of money and the analysis of credit which makes it possible to speak of a "monetary theory of credit," even if Marx's analyses on such points as the banking system and the balance of payments are more stimuli to thought than constituent elements of a completed theory.

Marx distinguishes "the monetary system" from "the credit

system" and "the monetary economy" from "the so-called credit economy," which he nevertheless calls "only a form of the monetary economy."[51] But "in developed capitalist production, the monetary economy no longer appears except as the basis of the credit economy."[52] One can then ask oneself if the important thing is not to examine the differences between the monetary and financial mechanisms to arrive at a theory of credit money. There being none, the principle of a monetary theory of credit is established in *Capital*. It is not that Marx holds a monetary theory of credit in spite of the difference between credit and money; on the contrary, the distinction between the two permits Marx to include credit in his general theory of money. The method followed in *Capital* defines itself negatively by the rejection of two temptations: that of a purely monetary analysis which would make credit only a surface expression of an eternal monetary essence, and that of a purely financial analysis which would examine credit solely in terms of the capitalist economy. Neither of these analyses would take into consideration the theoretical results developed in the examination of money and the circulation of capital. The "credit system" is the child of capitalist production *and* monetary circulation.

A. THE STRUCTURES OF CREDIT

In Volume III of *Capital* Marx returns to the question of credit a number of times. The place he assigns to loans and the lenders of money-capital is clearly indicated in a digression in a discussion of financing:

"The circulation of commodities always requires two things: commodities which are thrown into circulation, and money which is likewise thrown into it."[53] This phrase obviously refers to the general theory of money.

The "special conditions" of the reproduction of the social product are subject to "the general law. . . by which the money which the producers of commodities advance into circulation returns to them when the circulation of commodities takes place normally." (This is in regard to the financing of reproduction.)

From which it incidentally follows that, if behind the producer of the commodities himself there is a financial capitalist who in turn advances money capital (in the strictest sense of the word, capital value in the form of money) to the industrial capitalist, then the exact point to which that money will flow back is the pocket of the financial capitalist. Thus although money passes more or less through everybody's hands, the mass of the money in circulation belongs to the department of finance capital, concentrated and organized in the form of banks, etc. It is the way in which it advances its capital which, in the last analysis, produces the constant return of that capital to it in the form of money, although this process is in turn made possible by the reconversion of industrial capital into monetary capital.

This third point, "incidental" in the context of the system of reproduction, is fundamental in introducing the analysis of the structures of credit.

Marx is here about to put the *third stage* of his monetary theory, the "system of credit," in place. He has already indicated that credit functions in a *circular* pattern, and has at the same time shown that the relations between money, money-capital, and credit depend on the *specific relationships* between economic agents, with the capitalist class here divided into industrial capitalists and financial capitalists, who share the surplus value. The majority of the constituent elements of the monetary theory of credit have thus already been introduced before being brought together again in Part V of Volume III of *Capital*. The same is true of the idea of *financial capital*, referred to in the passage cited above and defined in Chapter XIX of Volume III.

Financial capital is money-capital, a fraction of total capital. But it is money-capital functioning "autonomously" to provide the financing of capitalist operations: its "capitalist function consists exclusively in performing these operations for the entire class of industrial and commercial capitalists."[54]

A technical division of labor takes place between the capitalists who take charge of the financial function and industrial capitalists. It reflects the role of money-capital in the circulation of capital, but is never total, "Because a part of the technical operations connected with money circulation must be carried out by the dealers and producers of commodities themselves."[55]

The financial function of financial capital is derived from that of money-capital. "The various operations, whose individualization into specific businesses gives rise to the money trade, spring from the different purposes of money itself and from its functions, which capital in its money-form must therefore likewise carry out."[56] This explains why credit can only be discussed *after money and money-capital.*

The technical division of labor between financial and industrial capitalists assigns the money-lenders the function of centralizing and redistributing the money available for the financing of production. But these "financial intermediaries" are capitalists; that is, it is only in their interest to undertake the technical performance of financial functions insofar as they profit by it as the result of a division of surplus value. After analyzing the formation of a general rate of profit ("average rate of profit"), and the "transformation of the values of commodities into prices of production," Marx discusses the "division of profit into interest and profits of enterprise" in Section V of Volume III, the part of *Capital* devoted to credit. Here the technical and economic aspects of the financial machinery of credit are combined.

I think that it is necessary to adopt a different order than that of the chapters of this section. A discussion of the structures of credit in conformity with Marx's general method should first show what the "system of credit" means in relation to the "monetary system" before analyzing the capital markets and the ways in which profit is divided between industrial and financial capital. Indeed, we shall see that the *monetary theory of credit* as conceived by Marx leads to a *unitary concept of credit* which includes the financial structures (markets and credit institutions) and their cyclical role in an interpretation tied to the unique properties of money and money-capital. One of the consequences of this concept is that financial capital participates in the division of an annual average rate of profit which is already *given,* and not in the *formation* of the average rate of profit; this can be understood and justified only in the context of a systematic discussion of the monetary characteristics of credit.

a. A Monetary Theory of Credit

1. Marx's method. Marx examines the "credit system" in the context of the capitalist form of production, where "capital has established its sway over production and imparted to it a wholly changed and specific form"[57] from that under other systems. The question, then, is not one of credit in general but of its role under specific conditions. "On the whole, interest-bearing capital under the modern credit system is adapted to the conditions of the capitalist mode of production."[58]

On a number of occasions Marx points out that "merchant's capital," that is, commercial capital and interest-bearing capital, historically preceded and in part created the conditions for the capitalist form of production. "Interest-bearing capital, or usurer's capital, as we may call it in its antiquated form, belonging together with its twin brother, merchant capital, to the antediluvian forms of capital, which long precede the capitalist mode of production and are to be found in the most diverse economic formations of society."[59]

Thus the medieval usurer, who is to the merchant as the financial capitalist is to the industrial capitalist, "converts his hoard of money into capital for himself"[60] according to the formula applicable to all capital, M-M', with the surplus m being in this case interest.

Because credit has this double aspect, ancient and modern, its study presents the same methodological problem as did that of money, with the same kind of solution, though in an inverted form. Marx constructed a general theory of money *before* analyzing the role of money in capitalism. He separated the discussion of simple circulation from that of the capitalist mode of production, in which on the one hand circulation has seized hold of production, while on the other, the process of production has absorbed circulation as one of its phases.[61] Inversely, he now takes as the subject of his examination "the modern credit system," corresponding to the capitalist mode of production and therefore having such specific structures as paper money, financial markets, etc. Yet interest-bearing capital is as old as commercial production, since "it requires no other condition for its existence . . . outside those necessary for the simple circulation of money and commodities."[62] Marx speaks of "merchants' capital" in his notes on "pre-capitalist conditions,"[63] after having a first historical survey in another chapter,[64] but he only gives a general theoretical treatment to the functioning of the credit system proper in modern capitalism.

The method followed in the two cases has the same dual character, in that the primitive forms of money and credit are differentiated from their function in the capitalist mode of production, while the "credit system" is only analyzed in capitalism. Marx has given a dual solution to the same methodological problem, reversing the order of its elements, since in the theory of money the analysis deals with the primitive form of the monetary system, while the theory of credit deals with the developed form of interest-bearing capital, the credit system.

This inversion takes place because it is impossible to understand the function of credit in the capitalist mode of production by considering it as merely the modern form of merchants' capital. There is a real break when merchants' capital is incorporated into the capitalist form of production and "functions only as an agent of productive capital."[65] This has been shown in the examination of the circulation of capital. Since the "modern credit system" has no meaning except in relation to the financing of capitalist reproduction, it becomes one of the elements of the new mode of production. Past forms of financial capital cannot serve as the starting point for the discussion of credit in the capitalist mode of production. But if it is impossible to start with the examination of ancient forms of interest-bearing capital, it is also a mistake to view "commodity-capital and money-capital, and later commercial capital and money-dealing capital as forms arising necessarily from the process of production as such, whereas they are due to the specific form of the capitalist mode of production which above all presupposes the circulation of commodities, and hence of money, as its basis."[66]

This would be to confuse all commercial production with capitalist production.[67] That is why it is necessary to study the structure of the "credit system," which is not just a technique for financing production. It is necessary to see how the *capitalist conditions, in which financial capital functions in a specific way, preserve the commodity basis of the whole system, and hence its "monetary basis."*

The preservation of this basis explains the survival of the practice of usury in the modern credit system.

Usury as such does not only continue to exist, but is even freed, among nations with a developed capitalist production, from the fetters imposed upon it by all previous legislation. Interest-bearing capital retains the form of usurer's capital in relation to persons or classes, or in circumstances where borrowing does not, nor can, take place in the sense corresponding to the capitalist mode of production; where borrowing takes place as a result of individual need, as at the pawnshop; where money is borrowed by wealthy spendthrifts for the purpose of squandering; or where the producer is a non-capitalist producer, such as a small farmer or craftsman, who is thus still, as the immediate producer, the owner of his own means of production; finally where the capitalist producer himself operates on such a small scale that he resembles those self-employed producers.[68]

Usury survives "in the pores of production" under capitalism. But that survival is only possible because of the existence of what Marx calls the "monetary basis" of the credit system itself. Just as the interdependence of the industrial capitalist and the financial capitalist corresponds to the different phases of the circulation of capital, so the mutual dependence of credit and money, based on the role of money as "general equivalent" and on the law of value, corresponds to the differences between the "monetary system" and the "credit system." That is why the analysis of the specific structures of credit takes place in terms of a monetary theory of credit which makes it possible to understand such survivals as usury, and the disturbances of the modern credit system itself which take place in the course of the cyclical changes discussed further on.

2. "Credit money." Following Tooke, and unlike Ricardo and the "Currency School," Marx distinguishes convertible banknotes from money proper (gold and substitutes for gold). Nevertheless such instruments of credit are themselves a medium of circulation, subject to the general laws of circulation: "We have already demonstrated in the discussion of the simple circulation of commodities (Volume I, Chapter III, 2), that the mass of actual circulating money, assuming the velocity of currency and economy of payments as given, is determined by the prices of commodities and the quantity of transactions. The same law governs the circulation of notes."[69] "Hence only the requirements of business itself exert an influence on the quantity of circulating money—notes and gold."[70]

These two points, the difference between money and banknotes and the monetary character of the latter, must be examined in turn. To understand their relationship is to see that the main distinction Marx makes is that between the "monetary *system*" and the "credit *system*," and that this distinction has meaning only in terms of a *momentary theory of credit money*. In this respect among others Marx's ideas part company not only with those of Ricardo but in part with those of Tooke, from whom he nevertheless borrows much of his description of the credit system.

The paper currency issued by banks has its origin in the credit instruments used by merchants and industrialists. The credit system includes acceptances, bills of exchange, banknotes, and checks—in short, *all evidences of debt*, whether used only between merchants or monetized by the banks and used as a medium of circulation. Nevertheless, it is necessary to distinguish, within this single system, between "commercial credit, that is, the credit which the capitalists engaged in reproduction grant one another," and "banking credit, which constitutes another, quite different, element."[71] The first "forms the basis of the credit system. Its representative is the bill of exchange, a certificate of indebtedness whose payment is due on a certain date,"[72] which can circulate from one merchant to another by endorsement without any intervening discount. This commercial credit, "the natural basis of the credit system,"[73] has its own roots in simple circulation, when money acquires the function of means of payment, with the seller becoming the creditor and the buyer becoming the debtor.[74]

"Credit-money springs directly out of the function of money as a means of payment. Certificates of the debts owing for the purchased commodities circulate for the purpose of transferring these debts to others. On the other hand, to the same extent as the system of credit is extended, so is the function of money as a means of payment."[75]

Commercial credit is thus on the borderline between the monetary system and the credit system. Incorporated into the latter, it introduces into it the contradiction inherent in the function of money as a means of payment,[76] which represents simultaneously the ultimate dematerialization of money and its re-embodiment.

The dematerialization of money manifests itself in the substitution for simultaneous exchanges of commodities and money of "legally executed private contracts" between creditors and debtors, in which money only makes its appearance as the measure of value in fixing the prices of the commodities sold, and hence as the measure of the debtor's obligation; the juridical and contractual character of the debts is here inextricably bound up with the economic function of money. To the extent that the payments balance, money does not make its appearance, just as if there were a pure system of commercial credit in which the accounts of the merchants and producers were in a state of equilibrium, with all financial transactions canceling one another out completely.

"Spinner A, for example, has to pay a bill to cotton broker B, and the latter to importer C. Now, if C also exports yarn, which happens often enough, he may buy yarn from A on a bill of exchange and the Spinner A may pay the broker B with the broker's own bill which was received in payment from C. At most, a balance will have to be paid in money."[77]

If the series of transactions ended in complete compensation, there would be neither the contradiction of money as means of payment nor money at all—once the monetary prices of the commodities had been initially fixed. But Marx immediately points out the limits of commercial credit[78] and thus reintroduces *in the credit system a demand for money in the shape of a need for "ready cash."* The circuit is in fact never completely closed, and so "This credit system does not do away with the necessity for cash payments. For one thing, a large portion of expenses must always be paid in cash, e.g., wages, taxes, etc. Furthermore, capitalist B, who has received from C a bill of exchange in place of cash payment, may have to pay a bill of his own which has fallen due to D before C's bill becomes due, and so he must have ready cash. A complete circuit of reproduction as that assumed above, i.e., from cotton planter to cotton spinner and back again, can only constitute an exception; it will be constantly interrupted at many points."[79]

Because of the diversity of the branches of production, the totality of transactions between capitalists cannot constitute a complete circle of debts with a balance of zero left over. "For example, the claim of the spinner on the weaver is not settled by the claim of the coal-dealer on the machine-builder. The spinner never has any counter-claims in his business on the machine-builder, in his business, because his product, yarn, never enters as an element in the machine-builder's reproduction process. Such claims must, therefore, be settled by money."[80]

It is also necessary to take into account the due dates of the obligations and the fluctuations in the salability and prices of commodities; these also create a need for cash in hand. The circuit of commercial credit can never be entirely closed without any use of cash. Gaps occur, and money reappears as the general equivalent to settle the transactions; its function as means of payment now involves the presence of cash, the re-embodiment of money.

If it is gold that serves as the means of payment, money presents itself in a material form adequate to its function. At the same time it cancels out the credit transaction which it has completed. But in the context of the credit system, gold may be replaced by banknotes which "do not rest upon the circulation of money, be it metallic or government-issued paper money, but rather upon the circulation of bills of exchange."[81]

"A bank note is nothing but a draft upon the banker, payable at any time to the bearer, and given by the banker in place of private drafts. This last form of credit appears particularly important and striking to the layman, first, because this form of credit-money breaks out of the confines of mere commercial circulation into general circulation and serves there as money. . . ."[82]

The problem, then, is to know how to define the *monetary characteristics* of this "credit money," whose basis is the circulation of debts, that is, *a non-circulation of money.*

According to Marx, it is just because credit money is part of the credit system and differs completely from gold, that it obeys the general laws of monetary circulation and thus becomes "money." If credit money were confused with gold, the quantity of notes issued by the banks would depend on the amount of gold needed to satisfy the requirements of circulation. This would make the given quantity of gold the keystone of the entire means of payment, including the monetary system and the credit system without distinction, in accordance with Ricardo's concept. In contrast, *to differentiate credit money from gold is not to remove the latter from the laws of monetary circulation; on the contrary,* from Marx's anti-quantitative viewpoint, *it is to subject it to them.* The movement of the medium of circulation depends on the needs of the economic agents, that is, on their demand for money. The bankers are no more able than the producers of gold to force the effective circulation of an amount of money greater or smaller than that for which there is a demand. The difference between the amount of money produced or issued and the amount needed for effective circulation always corresponds to a hoarding or dishoarding.

The "credit money" implicit in the credit system then necessarily has monetary characteristics analogous to those of gold; it is not only a medium of circulation, but an instrument of hoarding. On this point Marx parts company with Tooke and Fullarton who, according to him, did not know how to analyze in the abstract the way in which the monetary characteristics of a money are constituted,[83] and did not properly understand the significance of the demand for banknotes as a demand for "means of payment."[84]

Nevertheless, the first function of money, that of the measure of values, cannot be directly fulfilled by credit money. In that sense, "credit money" is only "money insofar as it absolutely takes the place of actual money to the amount of its nominal value."[85] But this convertibility has only theoretical significance; in normal times it does not in any way imply an effective convertibility, since banknotes are not symbols of gold but monetized debt. That is why "Note circulation is just as independent of the state of the gold reserve in the vaults of the bank, which guarantees the convertibility of these notes, as it is of the will of the Bank of England."[86] That is also why, as we shall see later, Marx criticizes the monetary policy inspired by Ricardo which limits the circulation of notes in relation to the size of the gold reserve. Under these conditions, what significance is there to the maintenance of the principle of convertibility? I think that for Marx it only means that the determination of monetary prices depends originally on the function of the money commodity as measure of value. But that initial determination does not cover either the formation of the relative prices of commodities, taking into account the average rate of profit, or the cyclical variations of relative prices and the general price level. The problem of prices is not, for Marx, a monetary problem,[87] once the origin of the general equivalent has been established. The maintenance of the *principle* of convertibility serves to preserve the primitive role of money as measure of value. But except in a credit crisis, that principle is not *applied*, because the economically important variations of prices under capitalism do not depend on the variations in the value of gold (which is postulated), but on the contrary the circulation of all money is itself dependent on prices. For these reasons it seems to me pointless to defend Marx's monetary theory, as H. Denis has done in his book on money,[88] by showing that the movements of prices from 1820 to 1914 were tied to the variation of the price of gold. This method neglects all the intermediate steps introduced in *Capital* between the initial determination of monetary prices and the determination of the variations of these prices under the capitalist system. It is not only pointless but dangerous, since it can indirectly open the way to Ricardo's ideas if we follow the advice of Wicksell,[89] who recommended that the theory of the cost of production be made an element of the Quantity Theory of Money.[89]

According to Marx "credit money," convertible in principle, has in the last analysis all the characteristics of a money although it initially develops as a non-money. That is why the credit system preserves as its foundation the monetary system for which it is a substitute. The laws of the circulation of commodities, adapting themselves to the specific financial conditions of the capitalist mode of production, inevitably remain valid. Where there is production of commodities, there is circulation of money; if credit replaces money, it is because it has monetary characteristics, which can brutally reveal themselves as such in a period of crisis. Contrary to what one commentator on Marx's monetary theory says,[90] even well-planned production would not permit the complete elimination of money by credit, if it remained a production of commodities; its instruments of circulation necessarily take the character of money.

The monetization of debts by the banks, examined so far in terms of the monetary theory of credit, translates itself in the balance-sheets of the banks into a list of assets which includes the commercial loans and a list of liabilities which includes the banknotes. But the banks are not pure issuers of money, meeting technical needs, but also capitalist institutions carrying on the money trade and having a loan capital available for this purpose. This, says Marx, is "the other side of the credit system,"[91] which must now be discussed. But the two aspects are linked; his monetary theory leads Marx to a unitary concept of credit. Unity of capital markets, a single rate of interest, complementary character of financial circuits: all these concepts which are used today, for instance, by the French National Accounts in studying the total supply and demand for capital, are to be found in Volume III of *Capital*. But since, according to Marx, the unity of the financial system depends logically on the monetary basis of credit, it is simultaneously indestructible and fragile, continually reconstructing itself from its own ruins. This double aspect, to be seen in the examination of the structures of credit, will reveal itself completely in the discussion of cycles.

b. A Unitary Concept of Credit.

The implications of the "monetary theory of credit" are far from being systematically developed by Marx. In order not to exaggerate the cohesion of the material on this question in Volume III of *Capital*, I prefer to speak of the unitary "concept" of credit which flows from the monetary theory.

1. Unity of capital markets and of the rate of interest. In certain passages, Marx deals with the different aspects of the capital markets, distinguishing between the financial market for long-term loans and the monetary market for bank credit.[92] But in his analyses he subordinates these differences to a fundamental unity of the market for monetary resources, where the supply comes mainly from financial capitalists, including the banks; for a certain price, the rate of interest, they satisfy the demand of the industrial capitalists for money. This financing mechanism, which implies a division of the capitalist class, is the consequence of the relations already analyzed between commodities and money, productive capital and money capital, industrial capital and financial capital. It is based on the commodity supplied and sought in it, money, and it underlines the significance of Marx's use of the word "system" to characterize the modern organization of credit.

Financial capital, we have seen, is money capital devoted to financing operations; historically, these developed from the trade in gold and that in foreign exchange.[93] Before the formation of the credit system, "This circulation of money itself, a phase in commodity-circulation, is taken for granted in money-dealing. What the latter promotes is merely the technical operations of money-circulation which it concentrates, shortens, and simplifies."[94]

Modern credit renders analogous technical services. It reduces the costs of circulation, and "accelerates the phases" of the circulation of commodities and capital.[95] But its technical role can be fulfilled only in the context of a system based on the concentration of the monetary resources needed to satisfy the demand of the capitalists who need to monetize debts or borrow for long terms. Marx examines mainly:

the money-capital on the market . . . the available loanable capital in general.

In the money market only lenders and borrowers face one another. The commodity has the same form—money. . . . Moreover, with the development of large-scale industry, money-capital, so far as it appears on the market, is not represented by some individual capitalist, not the owner of one or another fraction of the capital on the market, but assumes the nature of a concentrated, organized mass, which, quite different from actual production, is subject to the control of bankers, i.e., the representatives of social capital. So that, as concerns the form of demand, loanable capital is confronted by the class as a whole, whereas in the province of supply it is lonable capital which obtains en masse.[96]

The unity of the capital markets thus rests on the form of the commodity whose supply and demand it brings together, on the function of the agents of that supply and demand, and finally on the centralizing role of the bankers who, serving as intermediaries, "confront the industrial capitalists and the commercial capitalists as representatives of all money lenders. . . . A bank represents a centralization of money-capital, of the lenders, on the one hand, and on the other a centralization of the borrowers."[97]

"The credit system, which has its focus in the so-called national banks and the big money-lenders and usurers surrounding them, constitutes enormous centralization" of monetary funds by a part of the capitalists, who "are augmented by financiers and stock jobbers."[98] Given all these constituent elements of the credit system, the differences between the types of credits and loans, short or long term, are secondary in comparison to the unity of the market in monetary resources.

oans, short or long term, are secondary in comparison to the unity of the market in monetary resources.

But this unity of the credit system rests on the division of the capitalist class into financial capitalists, characterized by Marx as "parasites" and "honorable bandits,"[99] and industrial capitalists. It is this which leads to the existence of the rate of interest, deducted by the lenders from the profits of the "active capitalists"; the profits of the banks come from the difference between the rate at which they borrow and the rate at which they lend.[100] In general, Marx speaks of the rate of interest as a single category, without taking into consideration the differences between monetary rates and rates on the financial market.[101] It would be going too far to deduce from this, as Fan Hung does,[102] that Marx, like Keynes later, considers interest a monetary rate whose "determination . . . is specifically a monetary problem." It nevertheless remains true that in *Capital* the category of the rate of interest rests principally on the analysis of the supply and demand for monetary resources which are distinct from "real capital" just as money is distinct from commodities, money-capital from productive capital—and the financial capitalist from the industrial capitalist. In this sense one can, with Fan Hung, speak of a monetary theory of the rate of interest in *Capital.*

Like the concept of the credit *system*, the *category of the rate of interest* implies an analysis of the relation between financial capitalists and industrial capitalists. Credit is obviously an aid in the accumulation of industrial capital. The limits within which the individual capitalist has money-capital available by means of self-financing are transcended "thanks to credit."[103] The same is true of the monetary limits of social accumulation: "This disposes also of the absurd question, whether capitalist production in its present volume would be possible without the credit system (even if regarded only from this point of view), that is, with the circulation of metallic coin alone. Evidently this is not the case. It would rather have encountered barriers in the volume of production of precious metals."[104]

Furthermore credit, by increasing the mobility of capital, facilitates the equalization of the rate of profit in the different branches of industry.[105] The industrial capitalists thus need a credit system and derive profit from its existence—on condition that they reward the financial capitalists with a part of their profit.

The division of the average profit (determined elsewhere) into interest and entrepreneurial profit then depends only on the conditions of supply and demand on the market for monetary resources; it is thus competition, or the balance of forces between lenders and borrowers, which determines "the market rate of interest."[106] One can calculate "an average rate of interest" differing from the constantly fluctuating market rate if one calculates the average rates during the industrial cycles and "the rate of interest for investments which require long-term loans of capital."[107] But the determination of this average rate is also purely empirical: "There is no good reason why average conditions of competition, the balance between lenders and borrowers, should give the lender a rate of interest of 3, 4, 5 percent, etc., on his capital, or else a certain percentage of the gross profit. . . ."[108]

There is no general law "except that enforced by competition"[109] governing the division between interest and entrepreneurial profit "because it is merely a question of dividing the gross profit between two owners of capital under different title."[110] The sole preconditions of the division are then that the rate of interest cannot be zero, and that it cannot equal or exceed the average rate of profit. This contingent character of the rate of interest is tied to the special character of the capital market.

Monetary resources are not sold like commodities; there is no simultaneous exchange of equivalents. "In an ordinary exchange of commodities, money always comes from the buyer's side; but in a loan it comes from the side of the seller. He is the one who gives money for a certain period, and the buyer of capital is the one who receives it as a commodity. But this is only possible as long as the money acts as capital and is therefore advanced.[111]

Interest is not the price of capital. It does not express the intrinsic value of capital, for that depends on the value produced by the employment of the money-capital lent to the producers. Nor does it express the social scarcity of capital, since it merely reflects the inadequacy of the resources of the investors. It is then purely a form of division of the mass of the profit, such that its economic existence is shown only by its empirically determined rate. Marx goes so far in this reduction of interest to a simple diversion of the part of the profit that he does not take into account the risk, the calculations, and the expectations of the lenders and borrowers, all things that could give interest a special significance.

If the "quantitative" division of the profit nevertheless is transformed into a "qualitative" division, it is because of "the assumption, that the money-capitalist and the industrial capitalist really confront one another, not just as legally different persons, but as persons playing entirely different roles in the reproduction process, or as persons in whose hands the same capital really performs a two-fold and wholly different movement. The one merely loans it; the other employs it productively."[112]

Loan capital is "real" money in the hands of the borrower who puts it to productive use but a title to money for the lender who participates in the financing of production.[113] What appears as an antagonism in terms of the division of profit corresponds to the functional difference between productive capital and money-capital; the latter, though unproductive in itself, is an indispensable link in the circulation of capital. The category of interest simultaneously reflects the difference between self-financing and credit and that between all financing and production. Marx's Saint-Simonian way of brutally describing the financiers as "parasites" is explained by his whole theory of money and the role of money-capital.

One sees in what terms the unitary concept of the capital market is drawn. This unification can be considered as a rough sketch of the function of financing today as described by the National Accounts. But its other side is the failure to examine the effects of calculation and expectations on the decisions of lenders and borrowers. This gives a static character to the concept of speculation, to be defined further on.

It is the analysis of the role of the banks which, despite its incompleteness, is most interesting. For it incorporates the problem of money into that of financing in a new way. As a result, the unification of the credit system takes on a novel aspect.

2. Induction of the financial circuits. *The Banks.* The credit system has numerous ramifications, corresponding to the various types of credit (commercial, financial, monetary). All compete in supplying monetary resources. It is nevertheless necessary to analyze the way in which the different branches of the system complement one another. While preserving their differences (commercial credits, for example, are not credit money), the forms of credit are complete in themselves and can in part be substituted for one another, since their modes of circulation have common characteristics. For one thing, most credits circulate "in a circuit"; their creation implies their cancellation by repayment. For another, they all tend to break out of that particular form of circulation, to the extent that they are themselves commodities negotiable on the capital markets. Thus in the case of credit money, "the conditions governing the issue of money determine also its reflux,"[114] just as the creation of commercial obligations implies their liquidation. Nevertheless new circuits are continually being formed; they become entangled by the sale and purchase of obligations which have become commodities, in such a way that the financial system tends to grow by feeding on its own substance. These two aspects of the complementary nature of the circuits are reflected in the way the system of bank credit functions. The banks appear in turn as financial intermediaries underwriting the operation of a particular circuit, and as the machinery of a banking system with a tendency to become imprisoned in itself and lose its functional character. In a general way: "If the loaned capital is circulating capital, it is likewise returned in the manner peculiar to circulating capital. . . . But as for loan capital, its reflux assumes the *form* of return payments, because its advance, by which it is transferred, possesses the form of a loan."[115]

The basis of the circularity of credit operations is thus to be found in the productive capitalist's need and receipt of funds, that is, in the circulation of capital M. . .M'. Marx remains true to the order he has established between the different concepts; the cycle of capital and money-capital, loan capital and the banking circuit, are the successively assembled links in a chain of transactions.

Because of their centralizing role, the banks have at their

disposal a considerable mass of loan capital: rotating funds and reserve funds of industrial capitalists and merchants, deposits of financial capitalists, liquid savings, and temporarily unemployed money of all social classes.[116] Banking credit thus has as a solid base a social supply of monetary resources centralized by the banks. Indeed, "In countries with a developed credit, we can assume that all money-capital available for lending exists in the form of deposits with banks and money-lenders."[117] This centralization of funds by the banking system can only perpetuate itself because of the circularity of the system.

Just as there is a circuit of commercial credit which implies its own closing, that is, its liquidation by the offsetting of obligations and the payment of balances, so there is a banking circuit in which the notes issued to monetize debts return to the issuing banks. These notes return first as the means of payment, to cancel the debts of the borrowers. This is the "reflux," analyzed by Tooke and Fullarton before Marx. The banknotes can likewise return as deposits in the banks, so that the closing of the circuit does not involve its liquidation, but rather its indefinite continuance. In short, the mechanism of the banking circuit furnishes a substitute for the hoarding of newly mined gold engaged in by a section of the capitalists.[118] Just as the producers of gold are the permanent suppliers of metallic money to the capitalists, so the banking system remains indefinitely the creditor of the industrial capitalists as a whole. In a normal period, moreover, the total of centralized deposits remains stable, offsetting credit money in a way analogous to that in which the dishoarding of investors offsets the hoarding of capitalists setting up reserve funds:[119] "The deposits, unless tied up by agreement for a certain time, are always at the disposal of the depositors. They are in a state of continual fluctuation. But while one depositor draws on his account, another deposits, so that the general average sum total of deposits fluctuates little during periods of normal business."[120]

The consequence of these two processes, the deposit of the banknotes issued and the offsetting of deposits and withdrawals, is that the banking circuit can close and reproduce itself indefinitely by the continuous reconstitution of its financial base. The financing function of the various financial circuits can then be represented by the way one of these circuits, that of bank credit, functions. Its circular form and its manner of reproduction are similar to those of the majority of credit operations.

"On the basis of commercial credit, one person lends to another the money required for the reproduction process. But this now assumes the following form: the banker, who receives the money as a loan from one group of the reproductive capitalists, lends it to another group of the reproductive capitalists."[121]

The banker here only takes the place of one industrial capitalist, the "primary lender,"[122] in relation to another, the "deficitary,"[122] playing the role of a "financial intermediary,"[122] complementary to that of the primary lender; the basis of his activities is the primary credit relationship between industrial capitalists.

Nevertheless, only the bank can settle credit transactions in cash and put means of payment into circulation. Marx distinguishes between two types of banking activities, the monetization of debts and the advance of money-capital. The first is associated with a specific monetary interest rate, the second with a financial rate that depends on the total amount of loan capital in relation to the demand. Nevertheless these two different functions both involve the functioning of a financial *circuit*, and together they constitute the elements of the liabilities and assets of *the banking system considered as a whole*. That is why the consolidated balance-sheet of that system reflects the complementary nature of the multiple circuits of financing.

Up to this point the credit money issued by the banks has developed out of the general conditions of financing. The banker has given a monetary character to drafts on himself only as a substitute for direct obligations; his function has depended on the obligations contracted between producers and merchants, and on his own obligations to his creditors, the depositors. There has been no creation of money, but only the reconstitution by the bank of the monetary character of a whole collection of credits, when money has become lost in the relations of credit.

The bank's action has made the expansion of credits into a multiplication of the means of payment.

But the banking system is not merely an intermediary between depositors and borrowers; a bank also creates deposits by the credits it extends.[123] The complementary nature of these two activities shows itself in a tangle of composite elements which sometimes represent a social supply of loan capital and sometimes a purely banking supply of credit. Hence one part of banking assets rests entirely on banking activity itself and does not correspond to any liquid savings. Even more, these assets tend to become purely "fictitious"; Marx means by this that they tend to evade the conditions of the circulation of capital. Here the credit system takes on a third aspect.

In the same way as the circuit of commercial credit could be completely closed if there were complete compensation,[124] the circuit of bank credit could function as a closed circuit. In the banking system there is a true creation of deposits on the basis of the credits granted to borrowers. The tangible basis of the bank's liabilities, the supply of funds by the depositors, disappears when the banker lends "on overdraft" and, for example, opens a credit for the borrower which simultaneously inflates the bank's assets and liabilities. "The bank may open a credit account for A, in which case this A, the bank's debtor, becomes its imaginary depositor. He pays his creditors with cheques on the bank, and the recipient of these cheques passes them on to his own banker, who exchanges them for the cheques outstanding against him in the clearing house. In this case no mediation of notes takes place at all, and the entire transaction is confined to the fact that the bank settles its own debt with a cheque drawn on itself, and its actual recompense consists in its claim on A."[125]

Like circulating metallic money, credit money thus becomes "dematerialized" when it becomes a pure instrument of circulation, and its circuit is no longer closed by virtue of a compensatory hoarding, but as a result of its circular form alone.

The unity of the credit system then presents an altogether different aspect. Almost all banking assets take on a "fictitious" character when they circulate; their circulation becomes independent of that of "real capital" and even of the circular form which reflects, in terms of financing, the cycle of capital.

"Bank capital consists of 1) cash money, gold or notes; 2) securities. The latter can be subdivided into two parts: commercial paper or bills of exchange, which run for a period, become due from time to time, and whose discounting constitutes the essential business of the banker; and public securities, such as government bonds, treasury notes, stocks of all kinds, in short, interest-bearing paper which is however significantly different from bills of exchange. Mortgages may also be included here."[126]

Point 1, in regard to the reserve funds or cash of the banks, will be examined later. The monetization of commercial paper by the banks has already been discussed. We still must examine what Marx means when he speaks of the fictitious character of the public securities and the stocks held by the banks.

The public debt only represents "purely fictitious capital"[127] since the money-capital lent to the state has long since been spent by it. The obligations held by the creditors of the state represent an annual revenue; they can circulate in their own way by being sold to other individuals. But they cannot be canceled by repayment of the "principal." Because they do not represent any capital, that is, any "self-preserving value,"[128] they are not subject to either the movement of the circulation of capital, or the circular movement of the credit financing of productive activities. This kind of asset, animated by "its own laws of motion,"[129] can circulate indefinitely despite its "fictitious" character, or rather thanks to that character which preserves the public debt as such.

"The independent movement of the value"[130] of titles of ownership appears more clearly in the case of stocks which, unlike the public debt, represent "real" capital. "The stocks of railways, mines, navigation companies, and the like, represent actual capital, namely the capital invested and functioning in such enterprises, or the amount of money advanced by the stockholders for the purpose of being used as capital in such enterprises."[131]

These stocks have a nominal value, that of the amount of

money for which they were initially purchased. But as commodities which circulate in the stock market, they also have a price which depends on their rate of capitalization. Their market value "is in part speculative since it is determined not only by the actual income, but also by the anticipated income, which is calculated in advance."[132]

But, says Marx, even if the income of the business remained constant, or the annual payment was fixed by law, the market price of the "obligation" would vary inversely with the rate of interest: "Their value is always merely capitalized income, that is, the income calculated on the basis of a fictitious capital at the prevailing rate of interest."[133] The circulation of titles of ownership as stock market commodities gives them a "fictitious capital value" for everyone; "the money-value of the capital represented by this paper. . .is itself fictitious, in so far as the paper consists of drafts on guaranteed revenue (e.g., government securities), or titles of ownership to real capital (e.g., stocks), and that this value is regulated differently from that of the real capital, which the paper represents at least in part."[134]

The circulation of titles under the specific conditions of the financial market represents the past and future but never the present of the circulation of productive capital. "The greater portion of the banker's capital is, therefore, purely fictitious and consists of claims (bills of exchange), government securities (which represent spent capital), and stocks (drafts on future revenue)."[135]

The accumulation of bank capital then becomes purely a problem of the redistribution of the income created by industrial capital. To the extent that the financial system feeds on its own circulation, even in taking part in the financing of capitalist reproduction, it itself produces without limit—financial capitalists.[136] Its parasitical character is inseparable from its functional role.

Loan capital, by the very fact that it circulates, takes on a "fictitious" character. The circuit of credit, in enclosing itself completely within itself, reveals itself on a market of obligations which evades the conditions of the circulation of capital. From this point of view, the metamorphoses of banking capital represent those of the whole system of credit.

Marx says: "Even assuming that the form in which loan capital exists is exclusively that of real money, gold or silver—the commodity whose substance serves as a measure of value—a large portion of this money-capital is always necessarily purely fictitious, that is, a title to value—just as paper money."[137] All money which circulates dematerializes itself; all loan capital tends to become fictitious.

Marx insists on this point at length when, in opposition to Tooke, Fullarton, and MacLeod, he differentiates credit money and money-capital, issuance of instruments of circulation and loans of capital. How can these different elements be not only complementary but mixed up in a common process of dematerialization? This flows from the financial function of the credit system, which tends to put into circulation almost all the constituent parts of the system. Then a law of the monetary system, that of the dematerialization of the instruments of circulation, makes itself felt. In the same degree that the credit system evades the conditions of the circulation of capital, it becomes dependent on one of the general laws of simple circulation. Credit is undoubtedly an aid in the accumulation of real capital, but in its own way. One must not confuse loan capital and "real" capital any more than money and commodity.

"Everything in this credit system is doubled and trebled and transformed into a mere phantom of the imagination . . ."[138]— everything but the "reserve funds" of the banking system,[139] the first section of banking capital which we put aside a little while back, the only asset which corresponds to a real investment in liquidity on the part of the depositors.

"The reserve funds of the banks, in countries with developed capitalist production, always express on the average the quantity of money existing in the form of a hoard, and a portion of this hoard in turn consists of paper, mere drafts upon gold, which have no value in themselves."[140]

In spite of the absence of intrinsic value in this paper money, the significant thing here is its place in the reserve, its non-circulation. While all the other elements of the bank balance-sheets circulate, animated by a movement of their own, tangled up with one another, one part of bank capital does not circulate, and thereby preserves a tangible character. Thus the credit system, in its way, follows the same path as the monetary system: development on the basis of real transactions, dematerialization, then reconstitution of a solid element, the metallic reserve of the banks corresponding to a hoarding of liquid assets. That is why the reserve fund of the banks "contracts or expands in accordance with the requirements of actual circulation,"[141] just as hoarding of metallic money increases or diminishes as a function of the requirements of simple circulation.[142] Thus although the deposits multiplied or created by bank credits remain instruments of circulation, they cannot all circulate, lest the banker's credit be threatened along with his liquidity. Thus credit money obeys the general laws of monetary circulation; it only remains money if it does not circulate completely and continuously.

To finish with this point, one can say that the complementary nature of the financial circuits is reflected in the consolidated balance-sheets of the banks, which are at the same time issuers of money and lenders of money-capital. The function of the banks in financing rests on the circular character of banking operations, by virtue of which the banking system maintains and reproduces itself. At the same time a purely financial circulation develops; while it gives the credit system a "fictitious" character, it also preserves it as a financial system. Although the circuits of financing remain in the last analysis dependent on the needs of the productive capitalists, they can endlessly revolve confusedly about themselves, independent of the circulation of capital.

That is why credit, organized as a system, combines *even under capitalism* a composite of *pre-capitalist* elements (money and the money trade) and *post-capitalist* elements (the circuit of credit being "a superior circulation, effected by intermediaries, completed within itself, and already placed under social control").[143] *Though adapted to the needs of capitalism, credit is never really contemporaneous with capital.* The system of financing born of the capitalist form of production remains a bastard. And its "monetary base" makes its appearance when there is danger that it will be put out of service, whether it is a question of internal or international financial circuits. Before discussing this in detail in connection with the question of cycles, it is necessary to complete this analysis with an examination of the circuits of international payments.

The Balance of Payments and the "Demand for World Money." In terms of the monetary theory of credit, the reserve funds of the banking system are a means of hoarding. Their field of activity is both national and international. "Just as every country needs a reserve of money for its home circulation, so, too, it requires one for external circulation in the markets of the world. The functions of hoards, therefore, arise in part out of the function of money as the medium of home circulation and home payments, and in part out of its function of money of the world."[144]

Internal and international financial circuits complement each other. But the significance of this complementary nature must be examined with care, since on this point Marx is opposed both to Ricardo's ideas as a whole and to certain analyses of Tooke and Fullarton.

The discussion of the balance of payments and the demand for "world" money is placed *at the border between the structural and cyclical analyses of credit.* The latter analysis nevertheless remains in terms of the former except for the specifically cyclical question of speculation.[145] It is misunderstanding of the structure of the monetary system and the credit system that leads Ricardo to an erroneous analysis of the variations in the international circulation of gold. "I have shown by the example of Ricardo in what way their false conception of the laws that regulate the quantity of the circulating medium is reflected in their equally false conception of the international movement in the precious metals."[146]

Ricardo "asserts, for instance, that in periods of crop failure, which occurred frequently in England between 1800 and 1820, gold is exported, not because corn is needed and gold constitutes money, i.e., it is always an efficacious means of purchase and means of payment on the world market, but because the value of gold has fallen in relation to other commodities and hence the *currency* of the country suffering from crop failure is depreciated in relation to the other national *currencies.*"[147]

This erroneous concept of the interdependence of internal and international monetary circuits rests on the Quantity Theory of Money. According to Ricardo, the money in circulation becomes relatively overabundant in relation to commodities (here, wheat) and hence loses its own gold value. Thus it simultaneously de-values itself in relation to domestic commodities, whose prices rise, and to foreign currencies, in whose favor the exchange rate changes. Nevertheless monetary equilibrium is automatically re-established by the contraction of the national currency, whether by a decrease in the production of gold or by the export of gold (with a corresponding import of commodities). This concept, vigorously criticized by Malthus and by other economists, "ends by attributing to increases and decreases in the amount of pre-cious metals an absolute influence on bourgeois economy such as was never imagined even in the superstitious concepts of the Monetary System."[148]

The criticism of Ricardo's ideas by Malthus, Tooke, and Fullarton is taken up by Marx in terms of his general theory, according to which "increases or decreases in the amount of currency when the value of precious metals remains constant are always the consequence, never the cause, of price variations."[149] Two consequences flow from this and become *the premises of the cyclical analysis of financial mechanisms:* the amount of money in circulation in a country does not influence the rate of interest, which in general depends solely on the capital market,[150] and it does not influence the rate of exchange in a "normal" period (one without a crisis). On the contrary, the cyclical variations of prices influence the demand for money for commerce, whether internal credit money or specie. The mutual dependence of internal and international financial circuits, all subordinated to the banking machinery, changes the functional significance of the cycle. That is why, according to Marx, the international circulation of gold must be considered in the context of the world market, and in terms of a general financial cycle. This view is justified primarily because the financial cycle is only a reflection of the economic cycle; monetary and financial movements reflect non-monetary and non-financial internal and international disturbances. But they reflect them *in their own way* because of the existence of specific financial structures. Thus, although international commerce is only complementary to domestic commerce, "The balance of payment differs from the balance of trade in that it is a balance of trade which must be settled at a definite time";[151] one finds here, on another level, the mechanism which transforms commercial relations into a financial system. Consequently there is a specific demand for international money, different from the demand for internal instruments of circulation. But it is when the combined variations of the two affect the volume of the national store of gold that cyclical tensions influence both the internal credit system and international payments.

This is the logical sequence of Marx's analyses, scattered through numerous chapters of Volume III of *Capital*, but all dependent on his general theory of money and credit. It will then suffice to present Marx's comments in order, and to quote them at length.

Marx criticizes the procedure of starting with the excess money circulating in a single country and estimating its international effects, a method which misunderstands the meaning of monetary and financial phenomena. "It is characteristic of the English economic writers . . . that they look upon the exports of precious metals in times of crisis, in spite of the turn in the rates of exchange, only from the standpoint of England, as a purely national phenomenon."[152]

It is necessary at least to start by examining the mechanism of disequilibrium in *bilateral transactions*. For instance, if English cotton goods are exported to India and sold on credit, the balance of trade is favorable to England when Indian exports are smaller.[153] But the loan to India is an expenditure of English money-capital, with a corresponding import of obligations from India, that is, a debit for England. If colonial exploitation, the interest on English capital invested in India, and other sources of income in Indian money do not make up for the English debit, the English balance of payments is in deficit and must be settled by the export of gold. It is thus necessary to consider the balance of payments as a whole to understand the reasons for the export of gold. Even by starting from the single case of England and India, one sees the error of Ricardo's ideas on the exodus of gold, which is never due directly to a relative excess of money internally, and which thus does not have the effects imagined by Ricardo on the prices of commodities. The bilateral movements of capital exert pressure on the English and international financial markets, and thus on the rate of interest in England and the rate of exchange between the pound sterling and the Indian rupee; they can directly affect "financial" prices but not those of English commodities. And they also affect the Indian financial market.

Marx emphasizes that, in a period of cyclical stress, the disequilibrium of the English balance of payments is necessarily contagious.

It should be noted in regard to imports and exports, that, one after another, all countries become involved in a crisis and that it then becomes evident that all of them, with few exceptions, have exported and imported too much, so that they all have an unfavourable balance of payments. The trouble, therefore, does not actually lie with the balance of payments. For example, England suffers from a drain of gold. It has imported too much. But at the same time all other countries are over-supplied with English goods. They have thus also imported too much. . . . The crisis may first break out in England, the country which advances most of the credit and takes the least, because the balance of payments, the balance of payments due, which must be settled immediately, is unfavourable, even though the general balance of trade is favourable. This is explained partly as a result of the credit which it has granted, and partly as a result of the huge quantity of capital loaned to foreign countries, so that a large quantity of returns flow back to it in commodities. . . . The Crash in England, initiated and accompanied by a gold drain, settles England's balance of payments, partly by a bankruptcy of its importers . . . partly by disposing of a portion of its commodity-capital at low prices abroad, and partly by the sale of foreign securities, the purchase of English securities, etc. Now comes the turn of some other country. . . . England now has a return flow of gold, the other country a gold drain. . . .

The balance of payments is in times of general crisis unfavourable to every nation, at least to every commercially developed nation, but always to each country in succession, as in volley firing, i.e., as soon as each one's turn comes for making payments; and once the crisis has broken out, e.g., in England, it compresses the series of these terms into a very short period. It then becomes evident that all these nations have simultaneously over-exported (thus over-produced) and over-imported (thus over-traded), that prices were inflated in all of them, and credit stretched too far. And the same break-down takes place in all of them. The phenomenon of a gold drain then takes place successively in all of them and proves precisely by its general character 1) that gold drain is just a phenomenon of a crisis, not its cause; 2) that the sequence in which it hits the various countries indicates only when their judgement-day has come, i.e., when the crisis started and its latent elements come to the fore there.[154]

This long quotation shows why and how a financial crisis spreads. Because of its own disequilibriums, each country finds itself affected by the financial troubles of its partners. Nevertheless the international diffusion of financial troubles is "a question of time," a composite time which includes the distance between the place of production and the market where the product is finally sold, the delay between the delivery of the commodity and payment for it in cash, the difference between the original and final prices due to speculation, etc. This commercial and financial time only reveals its presence at the hour of settlement, when it is necessary to produce hard cash and pay all debts at the same time; it is then reabsorbed in a world financial space, plowed under by gold, the universal money.

The contagious character of financial troubles is characteristic of a cyclical crisis. In a normal period, there is a functioning international financial circuit which is a simple proportionate reproduction of the national financial circuits. The "gold and silver . . . distribute themselves once more in the proportions in which they existed in a state of equilibrium as individual hoards of the various countries. Other conditions being equal, the relative magnitude of a hoard in each country will be determined by the role of that country in the world-market."[155]

During a period of disequilibrium, in contrast, a complex tangle of overextended markets develops. The upsetting of one national balance of payments leads to similar problems elsewhere. Then the variations in exchange rates and the export of gold, without special importance in normal times, become the elements of an international financial crisis.

In a general way, "The foreign rates of exchange may change:

1) In consequence of the immediate balance of payment, no matter what the cause—a purely mercantile one, or capital investment abroad, or government expenditures for wars, etc., in so far as cash payments are made to foreign countries.[156]

2) In consequence of money depreciation—whether metal or paper—in a particular country. This is purely nominal. If one pound sterling should represent only half as much money as formerly, it would naturally be counted as 12.5 francs instead of 25 francs.[157]

3) When it is a matter of a rate of exchange between countries, of which one uses silver and the other gold as "money," the rate of exchange depends upon the relative fluctuations of the value of these two metals[158]

Variations in the rate of exchange depend mainly on a specific demand for foreign money for international transactions of all sorts. It is not an excessive internal supply of money which, by its effect on prices, explains the fall of English exchange at a given moment. Rather, it is the English demand for foreign money which, dependent on the state of the balance of payments, causes the pound to fall on the exchange market. Like Tooke and Fullarton, Marx differentiates between the demands for domestic and for international instruments of circulation and payment.

Marx does not speak of the system of the international gold standard, which was only developed after 1870, with the intention of stabilizing the rates of exchange of the various national currencies. But the analysis in *Capital* indicates clearly that in normal times variations in rates of exchange and international movements of the precious metals have little importance, whereas in a period of stress they inevitably have serious financial consequences, represented by the loss of gold by one nation after another. Since the export of gold is not the cause of the initial disequilibrum, it is also not the cause of the equilibrium finally attained by monetary deflation. It merely reflects on a monetary and financial plane a global crisis which is its own solution.

There is none the less a financial crisis, because of the existence of specific financial structures; the gold drain is only an index of the general crisis, but it is *gold* that is in demand at that particular moment. And under any circumstances it is gold which serves as "world money" to settle a balance of payments, and is *demanded* as such.

Nevertheless the mechanism of the banking *supply* of means of payment to settle debts is the same, whether it is a question of internal or international financial circuits. The banker is a money-changer.

"If the demand for money accommodation arises from an unfavourable national balance of payments and thereby implies a drain of gold, the matter is very simple. The bills of exchange are discounted in bank-notes. The bank-notes are exchanged for gold by the Bank itself . . . and this gold is exported. It is as though the Bank paid out gold directly, without the mediation of notes, on discounting bills."[159]

The national bank keeps custody of a common metallic reserve fund for the whole banking system; this serves as the basis of all banking operations.

The determination of the metal reserve of the so-called national banks, a determination, however, which does not by itself regulate the magnitude of this metal hoard, for it can grow solely by the paralysis of domestic and foreign trade, is threefold: 1) reserve fund for international payments, in other words, reserve fund of world-money; 2) reserve fund for alternately expanding and contracting domestic metal circulation; 3) reserve fund for the payment of deposits and for the convertibility of notes. . . . The reserve fund can, therefore, also be influenced by conditions which affect every one of these three functions.[160]

In a period of stress the reserve funds of the central bank become the focal point of the different circuits of capital, internal and international. But in general, as an instrument of hoarding, they serve on the one hand as the monetary basis of the internal currency circulation, and on the other as the guarantee of the country's international credit.

The internal supply of means of payment being thus consolidated, the amount of the reserves depends chiefly on the demand for gold as world money. "The inland market does not need any metal even now,"[161] at least when the credit system is functioning well. In contrast, on the world market the precious metal remains the real money, the universal general equivalent. It is simultaneously currency and money-capital. Exported as means of payment, it functions "as a valuable substance in itself, as a quantity of value. It is at the same time capital, not capital as commodity-capital, but as money-capital, capital not in the form of commodities but in the form of money (and, at that, of money in the eminent sense of the word, in which it exists as universal world-market commodity). It is not a contradiction here between a demand for money as a means of payment and a demand for capital. The contradiction is rather between capital in its money-form and capital in its commodity-form; and the form which is here demanded and in which alone it can function, is its money-form."[162]

In opposition to Tooke and Fullarton, who often confuse money and capital, Marx specifies that the gold demanded to settle an unfavorable balance is world money, with a specific character. Once again one finds the fundamental distinction between money and commodity, between money-capital and commodity-capital, a distinction here linked with that between national money and world money. Thus the problem of the balance of payments, a monetary problem, has two aspects: that of credit, and that of gold. The two only occasionally merge.

As the diverse functions of the single reserve fund show, there is a demand for world money which differs from that for domestic money. Hence despite the complementary nature of the financial circuits and their common basis in the national hoard, the external capital market can function with relative autonomy. Thus "An unfavorable rate of exchange, or even a drain on gold, can take place when there is a great abundance of money in England, the interest rate is low and the price for securities is high."[163]

Everything depends on the business cycle. When there is an outflow of gold, and at the same time the internal demand for money already exceeds the supply of loan capital, the interest rate rises and the exchange rate becomes unfavorable. The exchange can straighten itself out if the rise in the interest rate curbs the export of money-capital. Under these conditions, the gold standard plays a role and "The interest rate may affect the rates of exchange, and the rates may affect the interest rate. . . ."[164] But this reciprocal action of the capital markets is essentially dependent on the financial cycle. The latter does not act directly on the prices of commodities; it only determines the moments when "the movements of the interest rate adhere closely to those of the metal reserve and the rates of exchange."[165]

The examination of the financial circuits as a whole necessarily leads to the discussion of the financial cycle. The monetary theory of credit, being unitary, includes the cyclical analysis which will now be undertaken.

B. CREDIT AND BUSINESS CYCLE

Was Marx, often regarded as a mediocre monetary theorist, a "mediocre cyclical theorist?" H. Bartoli says: "Marxian theory, a theory of general equilibrium, makes it possible to investigate why the equilibrium is disturbed but seems not to work when it comes to finding out why the cycle is the form of development of capitalism."[166] It is indisputable that, as Bartoli says, Marx did not construct a theory of the business cycle; a negative proof of this gap is the multiplication of Marxist cyclical theories, all basing themselves on some passage in *Capital*. But if the cyclical disequilibriums described by Marx are not the regular fluctuations of the business cycle, neither are they the partial accidents of which

Bartoli speaks; they correspond to the manner in which capitalist structures function, and to the patterns of overall adjustment of different economic, financial, and political structures.

The examination of the financial cycle, which completes that of structures of capitalist financing, includes a number of comments on this point which I shall outline before discussing them in detail. *a*) Entirely external to itself, a simple combination of financial circuits adapted to the financing of capitalist reproduction, and at the same time entirely self-contained in the sense that it has its beginning and end in the special movement of the credit system; *b*) although the general crisis is not a monetary phenomenon, the financial crisis plays a role in the business cycle as a whole. But its effect is mainly of a financial nature; in temporarily making the credit system inoperative, it reconstitutes the system's monetary basis and enables it to serve again in the financing of capitalist reproduction; *c*) monetary policy has meaning precisely because of the double character of the business cycle and the financial crisis. If the financial system were only functional and confined to the financing of the economy, it would only be possible to take action on financial crises by a transformation of the form of production. If it were purely self-contained, monetary policy would have no economic significance.

Marx's very numerous descriptions of the financial cycle in Volume III of *Capital* are presented in great disorder, but they all rest directly on the monetary theory of financial structures. They make it possible to understand better both the role of crises and the general structural significance of the business cycle. The following quotation, which relates to mercantile capital and therefore in part to financial capital, is the best introduction to the cyclical discussion of credit:

In spite of its independent status, the movement of merchant's capital is never more than the movement of industrial capital within the sphere of circulation. But by virtue of its independent status it moves within certain limits, independently of the bounds of the reproduction process and thereby even drives the latter beyond its bounds. This internal dependence and external independence push merchant's capital to a point where the internal connection is violently restored through a crisis.

Hence the phenomenon that crises do not come to the surface, do not break out, in the retail business first, which deals with direct consumption, but in the spheres of wholesale trade, and of banking, which places the money-capital at the disposal of the former. [167]

a. The Financial Cycle

Financial movements initially only reflect those of the monetary circulation, which in turn are dependent on the circulation of commodities and capital. We have seen that the credit system develops with the monetary system as its foundation, and that the circulation of money is a prerequisite of "money-dealing." [168] The financial cycle is thus mainly dependent on the demand of the industrial capitalists and merchants for "ready cash." When production and incomes are growing, the amount of money in circulation which is used for the payment of income increases. At the same time transactions between capitalists make use of commercial credit without increasing the demand for resources. In a period of recession, in contrast, the demand for money for the payment of income falls, while the demand of the capitalists for means of payment increases. Marx says that "the demand for currency between consumers and dealers predominates in periods of prosperity, and the demand for currency between capitalists predominates in periods of depression." [169]

This is not, properly speaking, a reference to the financial cycle; the movements of monetary circulation adapt themselves to the demand for the medium of circulation, a demand which changes in meaning rather than volume as a function of the general cycle. A financial cycle as such only appears when one considers, not the demand for the medium of circulation, but the relation between the *demand* and *supply* of credit. Contrary to what Fullarton thinks, "It is by no means the strong demand for loans . . . which distinguishes the period of depression from that of prosperity, but the ease with which this demand is satisfied in prosperity, and the difficulties which it meets in periods of depression. It is precisely the enormous development of the credit system during a prosperity period, hence also the enormous increase in the demand for loan capital and the readiness with which the supply meets it in such periods, which brings about a shortage of credit during a period of depression."[170]

It is therefore necessary to examine the way in which the demand and supply of credit adjust themselves and the resulting changes in the interest rate. At the beginning of a period of expansion, commercial credit is plentiful and the demand for monetary resources is weak compared to the supply. The industrial capitalists do not have much need for the financial capitalists.

After the process of reproduction has again reached that state of prosperity, which precedes that of over-exertion, commercial credit becomes very much extended; this forms, indeed, the "sound" basis again for a ready flow of returns and extended production. In this state the rate of interest is still low, although it rises above its minimum. This is, in fact, the only time that it can be said a low rate of interest, and consequently a relative abundance of loanable capital, coincides with a real expansion of industrial capital. The ready flow and regularity of the returns, linked with extensive commercial credit, ensures the supply of loan capital in spite of the increased demand for it, and prevents the level of the rate of interest from rising. [171]

"An abundance of loan capital is available simultaneously with a great expansion of industrial capital."[172] At this stage of the cycle, financial fluctuations are absorbed in the economic movement as a whole.

But there are other cyclical phases when "the movement of loan capital, as expressed in the rate of interest, is in the opposite direction to that of industrial capital."[173] At the beginning of the cycle, before the recovery, when there is "contraction of industrial capital," the low level of the interest rate indicates a relative surplus of loan capital. At the end of the cycle, in a period of "abundant industrial capital," the rate reaches its maximum and thus indicates a shortage of money-capital, its scarcity in relation to the demand. There is thus a specific financial cycle which reflects the general cycle.

The relative independence of the financial cycle is shown by the differing variations of the rate of interest, associated with it, and of prices, associated with the general business cycle. The rate of interest depends solely on the capital market and on the conditions which at a given moment determine the relative strengths of lenders and borrowers and the division of the average profit between them. A rise in the interest rate, according to Marx, does not depend on an increase in the prices of commodities, and if it does not enter into the computations determining their net prices, it does not affect those prices. The price of commodities is distinct from the price of money, just as commodities differ from money.[174]

The specific character of the financial cycle means that it behaves in its own way within the general cycle. Its specific effect is linked to the functional character of the credit system, which enables capitalist production to develop and extend itself "beyond its own boundaries." The operations of the capital market and those of the commodity markets intersect at certain points in the cycle, since both are subject to the "speculation" which is rooted in the expansion of industry and commerce, develops through credit, and eventually merges with the specifically financial speculative operations.

For Marx, speculation has a very broad meaning, involving all the buying and selling of industrialists and merchants, whether they make material investments or put money into financial operations, stockpile goods or sell them immediately, etc. One of its bases in capitalist reproduction itself is long-term investment, which immobilizes capital without an immediate counterpart.

On the one hand pressure is brought to bear on the money-market, while on the other, an easy money-market calls such enterprises into being en masse, thus creating the very circumstances which later give rise to pressure on the money-market. Pressure is brought to bear on the money-market, since large advances of money-capital are constantly needed here for long periods of time.

And this regardless of the fact that industrialists and merchants throw the money-capital necessary to carry on their business into speculative railway schemes, etc., and make it good by borrowing in the money-market.

On the other hand pressure on society's available productive capital. Since elements of productive capital are for ever being withdrawn from the market and only an equivalent in money is thrown on the market in their place, the effective demand rises without itself furnishing any element of supply. Hence a rise in the prices of productive materials as well as means of subsistence. To this must be added that stock-jobbing is a regular practice and capital is transferred on a large scale. A band of speculators, contractors, engineers, lawyers, etc., enrich themselves. They create a strong demand for articles of consumption on the market, wages rising at the same time. . . . Hence excessive imports and speculation in this line of the import business. [175]

As Tooke had said, financial speculation has its origin in the general economic situation; the expansion of credit is the effect, before it is the cause, of the general speculation of industrialists and merchants.

In this context, financial speculation develops on its own level and feeds the financial boom by increasing the demand for money-capital and helping to raise the rate of interest. But it is necessary to make clear the significance Marx gives it. Originating in the specific area of credit operations, financial speculation is analyzed in *Capital* mainly in terms of its effects at a given moment on the division of the assets of all the capitalists, and the redistribution of resources among the capitalists. Undoubtedly Marx mentions the role of expectations in speculation for a rise or fall, whether of product commodities or security-commodities.[176] But he does not analyze expectations as such, or the way in which they determine speculative phenomena. In a general way, to borrow a definition from P. Dieterlen, "speculation includes all those choices which, being made for the sake of a use or a result which is not immediate, arise from an expectation."[177] But what interests Marx most—and one unquestionably sees here the static character of part of his analysis of financing—is the effect of speculative choices on the division of monetary resources. Financial speculation, conditioned by the particular term of credit operations and by a certain expectation in regard to the future, has immediate effects—pressure on the capital market and a new division of funds—which in Marx's eyes give it its real significance. Thus, unlike the industrial capitalist, who also speculates in his way, "the chevalier of credit discounts his notes as cavalry with which to expand his business and cover one dubious operation with another, not for the purpose of making a profit but in order to take over the capital of others."[178]

Favorable circumstances for this are offered by the general development, thanks to credit, of that speculation of which financial speculation is only a caricature.

Nevertheless, the relatively autonomous financial cycle only has an economic effect if the general circumstances set the stage for it, as we have seen above in the case of outflows of gold.[179] Thus "The drain of bullion, which created an independent money panic in April 1847, was . . . but a precursor of the crisis, and a turn had already taken place before it broke out," that is, the exchange had become favorable to England before the crash. And "In 1839 a heavy drain of bullion took place for grain, etc., while business was strongly depressed, but there was no crisis or money panic."[180] The financial crisis, characterized by the relative scarcity of money-capital, only occurs at certain stages of the cycle. It unfolds independent of the general movements of the cycle, but is only a mere episode in it. This strange behavior stems from the particular structures of the credit system. The financial system has its own rhythm and develops by itself, but "the accumulation of juridical titles to future production" has no economic guarantee except a good market for the actual production.

That is why the financial crisis has an ambiguous character. It is the moment of truth, when "an enormous quantity of . . . plain swindle . . . collapses."[181] But it makes it possible for the credit system to develop anew afterwards.

b. The Crisis and the Credit System

Marx differentiates the monetary crisis which is a phase of every industrial crisis from the crisis "which also is called a monetary crisis, but which may be produced by itself as an independent phenomenon in such a way as to react only indirectly on industry and commerce."[182] The monetary crisis of the first type involves the need for ready cash on the part of industrialists and merchants in difficulties, while the second type has as its "sphere of direct action . . . banking, the stock exchange, and finance." It can occur and end before the general crisis, of which it is nevertheless an indirect condition and consequence. But in all cases when a crisis temporarily puts the credit system out of action, there are simultaneous monetary and financial crises.

A credit crisis can, during a period of cyclical stress, be unleashed by miniscule events. If the relative scarcity of money-capital and the rise of the interest rate are major, the credit system becomes fragile and a marginal variation can suffice to unleash a financial crisis, and combine financial and general crises. The threshold of monetary sensitivity is then very low. And Marx indicates that expectations, so far neglected in the analysis of speculation, play a considerable role.

If credit operations are expanded rather than curtailed by the export of gold, the rise in the interest rate, and the raising of the central bank's discount rate (a point to which we shall subsequently return), it is because a cumulative phenomenon occurs as a consequence of general financial speculation resulting from pessimistic expectations.

> . . . as soon as somewhat threatening conditions induce the bank to raise its discount rate . . . the general apprehension spreads that this will rise in crescendo. Everyone, and above all the credit swindler, will therefore strive to discount the future and have as many means of credit as possible at his command at the given time. These reasons, then, amount to this: it is not the mere quantity of imported or exported precious metal as such which makes its influence felt, but that it exerts its effect, firstly, by virtue of the specific character of precious metal as capital in money-form, and secondly, by acting like a feather which when added to the weight

on the scales, suffices to tip the oscillating balance definitely to one side; it acts because it arises under conditions when any addition decides in favour of one or the other side. Without these grounds, it would be quite inexplicable why a drain of gold amounting to, say, five or eight million pounds sterling—and this is the limit of experience to date—should have any appreciable effect. This small decrease or increase of capital, which seems insignificant even compared to the seventy million pounds in gold which circulate on an average in England, is really a negligibly small magnitude when compared to production of such volume as that of the English.

But it is precisely the development of the credit and banking system, which tends, on the one hand, to press all money-capital into the service of production (or what amounts to the same thing, to transform all money into capital), and which, on the other hand, reduces the metal reserve to a minimum in a certain phase of the cycle, so that it can no longer perform the functions for which it is intended—it is the developed credit and banking system which creates this over-sensitiveness of the whole organism. At less developed stages of production, the decrease or increase of the hoard below or above its average level is a relatively insignificant matter. Similarly, on the other hand, even a very considerable drain of gold is relatively ineffective if it does not occur in the critical period of the industrial cycle.[183]

This passage, which sums up and completes the points developed above, seems to me essential: the special sensitivity of developed capitalist economies to phenomena which are doubly marginal—that is, relatively unimportant and not specifically capitalist—is due precisely to the way in which capitalism has been able to incorporate these phenomena and make them elements of its own development. This explains the nature and function of the financial crisis.

According to Marx, the crisis of the credit system represents a regression of the whole capitalist financial organization, a "sudden change of the credit system into a monetary system." From this point of view, the financial crisis and the monetary crisis merge; both deprive money of its function as medium of circulation and give it the character of the "absolute commodity."

"In a crisis, the antithesis between commodities and their value-form, money, becomes heightened into an absolute contradiction. Hence, in such events, the form under which money appears is of no importance. The money famine continues, whether payments have to be made in gold or in credit money such as bank notes."[184]

"Under conditions of advanced bourgeois production, when the commodity-owner has long since become a capitalist, knows his Adam Smith and smiles superciliously at the superstition that only gold and silver constitute money or that money is after all the absolute commodity as distinct from other commodities—money then suddenly appears not as the medium of circulation but once more as the only adequate form of exchange-value, as a unique form of wealth just as it is regarded by the hoarder."[185]

The "sudden change of the credit system into a monetary system" means that there is a contraction of the functions of money into just one, that of money as object of hoarding.

The credit system, which had relieved the internal economy of payments in metallic money, once more falls under the sway of gold and silver. "In the crisis, the demand is made that all bills of exchange, securities, and commodities shall be simultaneously convertible into bank money, and all this bank money, in turn, into gold."[186]

But this regression of the system is connected with the very conditions in which it developed. We have seen above how the system of credit, even while substituting itself for the monetary system, preserves a "monetary base" embodied in the gold reserve of the central bank. The crisis merely isolates this "monetary base," which in normal times is merely a condition of the circulation of credit money, as if in a caricature. The hoarding peculiar to a crisis, says Marx, no longer corresponds to an imaginary depreciation of the value of commodities, but to an effective devalorization of all commodities, commodity capital, and financial paper. "A part of the gold and silver lies unused, i.e., does not function as capital."[187]

Since this aspect of hoarding is peculiar to the crisis of credit, and to its capitalist conditions, the hoarding has a special function: it serves to restore the connection between the credit system, overdeveloped by speculation, and the real supply of money-capital for lending.

The banking system starts hoarding when its liquidity decreases too much, though the circuit continues to turn. "The appearance of rapid and reliable refluxes always keeps up for a longer period after they are over in reality by virtue of the credit that is under way, since credit refluxes take the place of the real ones. The banks scent danger as soon as their clients deposit more bills of exchange than money."[188]

The banks then hoard, in the sense that they refuse to lend. By doing so they unleash or increase the financial panic.[189] But they also tend to avoid the collapse of their own credit, and to preserve themselves as organs of the credit system. The hoarding by the banks, while it ties up the system, also helps to preserve it. It seeks to limit the credit supplied by the banks in accordance with the relative scarcity of loan capital supplied by the depositors.

As to the other participants in the financial crisis, Marx says that their demand for the means of hoarding results from the absence of credit. Even in a period of crisis it can be translated into an increase in the amount of money in circulation, if the increase of notes as a means of payment is greater than the decrease in the circulation of notes as a means of purchase.[190] The amount of money circulating then depends on the credit policy of the banks, which can alleviate or aggravate the crisis. The banks' margin of maneuver is, however, limited by the necessity of preserving a certain degree of liquidity. Hoarding as a refusal to lend then has a double function: *it ties up the credit system, but it preserves the credit of the banking system.*

Undoubtedly it is this hoarding by banks in a period of crisis that explains what Marx says in the following passage: "The absolute amount of circulation has a determining influence on the rate of interest only in times of stringency. The demand for full circulation can either reflect merely a demand for hoarding medium . . . owing to lack of credit . . . or it may be that more means of circulation are actually required under the circumstances, as was the case in 1857."[191]

Even when the interest rate in general depends on a given

state of the capital market, the latter being distinct from monetary circulation, it can in exceptional cases be affected by the quantity of money in circulation due to variations in bank credit. Since the financial crisis is also a monetary crisis, all circuits are momentarily merged as a result of the demand for liquid money. The rate of interest then depends on the scarcity of credit money and money-capital for lending. But this idea does not fit well with the analyses in Volume II which argue that credit restrictions do not necessarily affect the quantity of money in circulation, which in turn has no effect on the interest rate. From this point of view the discussion of the supply of bank credit lacks clarity.

In conclusion, the analysis of the financial crisis starts by showing the secondary role of that crisis in the business cycle as a whole: "what appears as a crisis on the money-market is in reality an expression of abnormal conditions in the very process of production and reproduction."[192] The hoarding in a crisis is only the reverse side of the failure to sell commodities and the cessation of investment which follow an excessive expansion of production and commerce. On the other hand, the financial crisis plays a fundamental role in the functioning of the financial system. It shows there that the capitalist form of production is unable to give an entirely functional character to the conditions under which it functions; the credit system preserves a relatively autonomous development. The resurgence of the monetary system in times of crisis is a sign of that autonomy, since the demand for money is completely outside the movement of real production. But the financial crisis also reduces the "fictitious" mushrooming of credits and restores the monetary basis of credit. As Fan Hung[193] says, Marx regards debts as themselves money only to the extent that they replace money (as means of purchase or of payment) *in proportion to its normal value.* The crisis, a brutal manifestation of the law of value, makes it possible for credit to further replace money in the financing of capitalist production. And monetary policy can help or hinder this spontaneous process.

c. Banking Policy and Money Power

"But if, on the one hand, it is a popular delusion to ascribe stagnation in production and circulation to insufficiency of the circulating medium, it by no means follows, on the other hand, that an actual paucity of the medium in consequence, e.g., of bungling legislative interference with the regulation of the currency, may not give rise to such stagnation."[194]

Every monetary policy, whether good or bad, has effects on the financial cycle, according to Marx. The effectiveness of intervention by the monetary authorities depends on the ability of the national bank to act, which rests on the centralization of the banking system and the relation between the national bank and the state. But it also depends on a good understanding of the specific character of credit.

There can be a monetary policy without a policy for the whole economy, because of the special character of money. Banking policy must nevertheless be adapted to the particular character of the credit system. If it confuses the monetary system and the credit system, as does the Bank Act of 1844, based on the ideas of Ricardo and the Currency School, it has harmful effects, and can transform a financial crisis into general bankruptcy for the sole benefit of some big bankers, speculating on the shortage.[195] The Bank Act regulated the operation of the Bank of England in such a way that the notes issued by the bank were almost completely covered by reserves in specie or gold ingots. A decrease in the reserve, e.g., through export of gold, automatically brought about a restriction of the note issue. The stresses on the financial market were then aggravated by a credit policy which misunderstood the special character of the system it was to regulate. And finally, the speculative hoarding of the great private banks in need of nationally valid banknotes get them by panic."[196]

In place of the erroneous policy of the Bank Act, Tooke advocated an increase in the discount rate, based on the special banking role of the Bank of England. Just as industrialists get monetary resources by discounting their bills of exchange, so private banks in need of nationally valid banknotes get them by rediscounting their bills of exchange at the national bank, which then plays the role of bank of banks. In raising the discount rate, the national bank influences the rate at which all the banks lend. This raises the price of credit, and can correct the speculative excesses in the supply and demand for money.[197]

Marx agrees with Tooke that the artificial limitation of banknotes aggravates the financial crisis instead of alleviating it. Since the centralized organization of credit in England makes it possible in time of crisis to use the national bank's own credit, "guaranteed by the credit of the nation,"[198] it is necessary in times of scarcity to increase the supply of banknotes so as to avoid the collapse of the system of payments and limit the effects of speculative hoarding. It is not because he supports the quantity theory that Marx favors a dishoarding of banknotes. Rather, it is because he thinks that this increase in supply compensates for a partly artificial scarcity, makes it possible to satisfy the increased demand for money, and preserves the special elasticity of credit in relation to metallic reserves.

On the other hand, Marx thinks that the rise in the discount rate recommended by Tooke runs the risk of aggravating speculation and producing the cumulative phenomena which create a financial panic. He therefore opposes it. But he thinks that it is inevitable because of the intrinsic limits of "good" credit policy, which can avert panic and bankruptcy but cannot eliminate either the crises of confidence which periodically disrupt credit nor the speculative activity of the banking system. Marx is obviously no more a monetary reformer than he is a Saint-Simonian reformist. The limits of monetary policy are clearly indicated by him.

By definition, no monetary policy can abolish the economic causes of financial stresses; the relative autonomy which makes it possible for monetary policy to have an effect also sets the bounds of its field of action. The narrow scope for action by the national bank in times of financial crisis represents the intrinsically limited character of all monetary policy.

The method of alleviating the crisis recommended by Marx, the increase in the supply of means of payment, implies the centralization of the banking system, whose pivot is the national bank. It is on the level of this central bank, which has a monopoly on the issuance of banknotes accepted throughout the country, and with which the gold reserves of all the banks are deposited, that banking policy can be a monetary policy. The central bank is from this point of view a part of the state apparatus. But this political role which gives the central bank its strength also gives it a great fragility.[199] The gold reserves it centralizes cannot fall too much, lest the "national credit" itself be endangered. That, says Marx, is why "The fear which the modern banking system has of gold exports exceeds anything ever dreamt by the monetary system, which considered precious metals as the only true wealth."[200]

The centralization of the metallic reserves gives them a central importance which makes them extremely sensitive to slight variations. The power of the central bank over the credit system is real, but also as strictly limited as that of the state over money.[201]

In addition, the central bank, a "semi-private" organism, can itself seek to profit from financial crises to increase its own power. "Nevertheless, the Bank of England, being a public institution under government protection, cannot exploit its power as ruthlessly as does private business."[202]

But because it is "a peculiar mixture of national and private banks,"[203] its function is ambiguous. Its strategy represents a compromise between public monetary policy and the private decisions of the possessors of money. The monetary power of the state is thus limited not only by that of private individuals, but by that of the banking system, whose center is nevertheless directly linked to the state apparatus.

The organic base of monetary policy, although real, is thus fragile. And even if the policy applied is a "good" public monetary policy, the central bank's room for maneuver remains limited by the monetary base of the credit system. This conclusion in regard to credit in the capitalist form of production is combined with that of the general theory of money and Marx's starting-point, the origin and significance of the general equivalent.

It is a basic principle of capitalist production that money, as an independent form of value, stands in opposition to commodities, or that exchange-value must assume an independent form in money; and this is only possible when a definite commodity becomes the material whose value becomes a measure of all other commodities, so that it thus becomes the general commodity, the commodity par excellence—as distinguished from all other commodities. This must manifest itself in two respects, particularly among capitalistically developed nations, which to a large extent replace money, on the one hand, by credit operations, and on the other by credit-money. In times of a squeeze, when credit contracts or ceases entirely, money suddenly stands as the only means of payment and true existence of value in absolute opposition to all other commodities. Hence the universal depreciation of commodities, the difficulty or even impossibility of transforming them into money, i.e., into their own purely fantastic form. Secondly, however, credit-money itself is only money to the extent that it absolutely takes the place of actual money to the amount of its nominal value. With a drain on gold its convertibility, i.e., its identity with actual gold, becomes problematic. Hence coercive measures, raising the rate of interest, etc., for the purpose of safeguarding the conditions of this convertibility. This can be carried more or less to extremes by mistaken legislation, based on false theories of money and enforced upon the nation by the interests of the money-dealers, the Overstones and their ilk. The basis, however, is given with the basis of the mode of production itself. A depreciation of credit-money (not to mention, incidentally, a purely imaginary loss of its character as money) would unsettle all existing relations. Therefore, the value of commodities is sacrificed for the purpose of safeguarding the fantastic and independent existence of this value in money.[204]

The capitalist form of production, which has been able to develop a credit system fitting its financial needs, is much more sensitive to monetary crises than previous forms of production. No monetary policy can prevent financial crises from occurring and playing their role of re-establishing money, the general equivalent, as a means of hoarding.

These analyses of *Capital* show that no money can be permanently a mere means of circulation, if it is to retain its credibility. In the credit system, hoarding has a preservative role. Unquestionably the "hunger for gold" when a developed and efficient banking system exists is often thought of by Marx as a real reversion to the beginnings of the capitalist system. But hoarding, which in times of crisis appears as a relic of the monetary system, is a condition for the survival of the credit system. *In this sense* the most advanced capitalist society always has with it its mercantilist past.

But nowhere in *Capital* does the theory of money expand into a monetary theory of the economy; it remains purely a theory of the monetary economy. Without it, one understands capitalism poorly, but through it one never understands just money.

POSTSCRIPT TO THE SECOND EDITION

When a manuscript has been published, or even simply completed, one often says to oneself: "Today, I would not write it that way." Some years later one has to say the same thing again, after having done research which makes clear in retrospect the weaknesses of the previous manuscript. But it is no longer possible to retouch the original text, which becomes a way-station on the road of research. *Marx on Money* is an essay, complementary to other studies already published or still in preparation; instead of retouching the text, it is better to try to put it in context. That is, to emphasize what today, after numerous lively discussions and a vision less restrained by practical social concerns, appear to be strong points which have stood the test, along with certain weaknesses.

The solid part relates primarily to the subject itself, which was previously largely unknown. *Marx on Money* shows that money is not a technical problem, a subject reserved for study by some specialists, or an area reserved for so-called "bourgeois" political economy. All who want to understand the whole contribution of Marx's historical materialism should read the first section of Volume 1 of *Capital*, where a theory of commodities and money is presented.

Readers can certainly be turned away by the difficulty of that section, where Marx uses a Hegelian terminology. But it is necessary to go through it, for without commodities and money, which crystallize value in particular forms, there is neither surplus value nor capital. One should then seek to know why and how Marx analyzes commodities and money which, although not peculiar to any particular form of production, are not purely economic relationships but social relationships. This last point is clear when one follows the discussion of the reproduction of money as general equivalent, an indispensable reproduction, which takes place through contradictions arising from the diversity of the forms and functions of money. Marx *breaks* decisively with Ricardo's economic theory here, as well as with all "bourgeois" economic theories.

Marx's concept of money is often treated as a simple concept of the money commodity, even as a "metallism" making gold the sole money, so that there would be no perceptible difference on this point between Marx and Jacques Rueff. In contrast, *Marx on Money* seeks to show the prime importance of the concept of *"general equivalent,"* and the special position of "the money form" within Marx's theory of commodities. That is why the analysis of the beginning of *Capital* is not invalidated by that of commercial and banking credit money in connection with Volume III, where Marx's notes on credit money in the capitalist form of production are gathered together. The examination of financial circulation shows that credit, while adapted to the needs of capitalism, "is never really contemporaneous with capital." Thus the formation and circulation of credit money cannot be considered as depending on what is today called a "function of financing," an expression which masks the compulsions and social, economic, and political contradictions associated with every use of money. *Marx on Money* has tried to pave the way to a "functional" and at the same time "voluntarist" interpretation of credit money, with state and central bank as "free suppliers" of money.

Nevertheless, this little book has its weak points, not all of which have as yet been eliminated by subsequent books and some of which are still the subjects of research.

In the first place, it is necessary to reconsider what is said in the introduction to justify the placing of the discussion of money at the beginning of *Capital*. It is written there that Marx followed this course for theoretical reasons. This remains true, but it seems to me today that the theoretical reasons are inseparable from historical considerations, from the fact that value, commodity, and money are *social processes*.

N.B.: This is by no means to adopt the interpretation of Engels, whereby value in exchange would be viewed as belonging to the period before the capitalist form of production, in which "prices of production" would appear. Such a break between value in exchange and price of production, which has now surfaced again in the neo-Ricardian school led by Sraffa, seems to have no basis. There is no longer a "mercantile form of production," but only "pockets" of mercantile production and circulation, of greater or smaller extent according to the various types of production. These are characterized by *special relations of production*. (The term "relations of production" is applied to the socio-economic relationships between direct producers, slaves, peasant serfs, and wage-workers on the one side and, on the other, those who are able to expropriate the products of the surplus labor of the first group in one way or another, surplus value being the form characteristic of the capitalist mode of production.) *On the contrary*, although elements of mercantile economy come into existence and reproduce themselves (e.g., mercantile exchanges of surplus products between various types of peasants and city dwellers, or between artisans and villagers, etc.), no relation of exploitation and dependence connected with relations of production can reveal itself directly. That is why the producers exchanging their products in mercantile production and circulation, of whom Marx speaks at the beginning of *Capital*, are considered as individual workers with equal rights to the possession of the commodities which they have themselves produced for exchange. This is a "good abstraction!"

Compulsions and *social contradictions* are no less present because the relation of exchange between independent producers is included in what Marx calls "a spontaneous organization of production whose threads have been woven and continue to be woven without the knowledge of the producers carrying on the exchanges." It does not matter that they are the free possessors of the commodities they exchange; *they nevertheless do not control the social process of production and exchange*. Hence its contradictory character, which shows itself particularly in the operation of a relative "valorization" or "devalorization" of commodities in comparison with each other, and an "appreciation" or "depreciation" of commodities in relation to money, in terms of the *"labor time socially necessary"* to produce commodities and money at a given time. The meaning of this *"law of value"* should have been explained at the beginning of *Marx on Money*. That would have avoided the risk of separating the "economic," the "social," the "historical," and even the "political," a risk present in certain formulations in the first part, at the beginning of point A and the end of point B, and not sufficiently compensated for by other formulations.

Moreover, the meaning of the disparity between the "market price" and the value of a commodity could have been presented more clearly. This leads to a more general point, which is not made in *Marx on Money* in spite of a brief critique of Paul M. Sweezy's ideas on "prices of production." This point, which has emerged in the course of further research by other Marxists as well as myself, and a number of joint discussions, is that there is in *Capital* no *general theory of prices* which would cover both the market prices at the beginning of *Capital* and the prices of production peculiar to capitalism, which Marx discusses in Volume III. Although the "price form" is clearly analyzed, as is shown elsewhere in *Marx on Money*, the formation of the various types of prices and their interconnection is never made satisfactorily clear. Nevertheless we do not know whether it is a question of a theoretical gap which Marx might have tried unsuccessfully to fill, or whether the problem is a false one! In the second case we would be speaking of the absence of a general theory of prices in *Capital* as if such a theory had a meaning and necessarily existed, although in reality we would be asking Marx a question arising from a "bourgeois" idea of the economy and meaningless from a Marxist perspective. True or false problem? The *present* state of studies on the question does not seem to me to permit an answer.

The second part of *Marx on Money* has a number of obvious weaknesses. In particular, the discussion of "the financial requirements of equilibrium," bound up with the discussion of the "balance-sheets" of the capitalists of Department I (production of production goods) and Department II (production of consumption goods), rests on an "uncritical" consideration of the idea of economic and financial *equilibrium*. It is true that this error is in part compensated for subsequently in the text, where it is pointed out that money, as a particular social relationship, is never "neutral" whether there is equilibrium or not. It is also clearly stated that the "credit system" does not have a merely functional character in relation to the financing of capitalism, and that it is necessary to analyze "financial cycles" and monetary crises with care. Nevertheless, a critical analysis of the concept of equilibrium and its theoretical implications was needed.

These are the principal things which it now seems to me need to be said in regard to *Marx on Money*. This essay, it must be repeated, is one stage on a long journey, in the course of which both errors and truths will necessarily be launched and subjected to criticism.

NOTES AND REFERENCES

INTRODUCTION

1. *Revue économique*, Jan. 1967.
2. David Ricardo, *The works and Correspondence of David Ricardo*, Vol. I, *The Principles of Political Economy and Taxation*, Piero Sraffa, ed. (Cambridge: Cambridge University Press, 1961).
3. Karl Marx, *Capital*, (New York: International Publishers, 1970), I, 80-81. All references to *Capital* hereafter are to this edition.
4. Louis Althusser and Etienne Balibar, *Reading Capital* (New York: Pantheon, 1970).
5. H. Denis, *La Monnaie* (Paris: Editions sociales, 1951).
6. John Maynard Keynes, *The General Theory of Employment, Interest and Money* (New York: Harcourt, Brace & Co., 1936).

PART ONE

1. R. Establet, *Reading Capital*, op. cit.
2. The discussion of Hilferding's book as a whole will be the subject of a subsequent work.
3. *Capital*, II, 116.
4. Ibid., II, 81.
5. Ibid., II, 112.
6. Karl Marx, *A Contribution to the Critique of Political Economy* (New York: New World Paperbacks, 1970), p. 187. Hereafter cited as *Critique* for all references to this edition.
7. Ibid. p. 65.
8. Ibid. p. 85.
9. Ibid. p. 170.
10. *Capital*, I, 92.
11. *Critique*, pp. 65-66.
12. *Capital*, I, 68-69.
13. Ibid., I, 67.
14. Ibid., I, 101-102.
15. Ibid., III, 193.
16. Ibid., I, 100.
17. *Critique*, p. 73.
18. Ibid., pp. 200 ff.
19. *Capital*, I, 118.
20. *Critique*, p. 164.
21. *Capital*, I, 123.
22. *Critique*, p. 160.

23. The market price is here the price at which a certain quantity of pieces of money can be exchanged against uncoined gold. This gold market, in simple circulation, has to do with the exchange of material metal; it is completely different from the money market associated with credit.

24. *Capital*, I, 125-126.

25. The theory of the balance of payments and foreign exchange will be examined in the second major part of this study. See pp. 144 ff.

26. Karl Marx, *The Poverty of Philosophy* (New York: New World Paperbacks, 1967), pp. 87-88.

27. H. Bartoli, *La doctrine économique et sociale de Marx* (Paris, 1950).

28. *Critique*, pp. 169 ff.

29. C. Rist, *Historie des doctrines relative au crédit et á la monnaie* (Sirey, 1951), pp. 170-171.

30. *Critique*, p. 185.

31. C. Rist, op. cit., p. 343.

32. *Critique*, p. 121.

33. *Capital*, I, 128.

34. J. M. Keynes, *The Pure Theory of Money*, vol. I of *A Treatise on Money* (New York: Harcourt, Brace & Co., 1930), pp. 146-147.

35. *Critique*, p. 119.

36. C. Rist, op. cit., p. 51.

37. C. Rist, op. cit., p. 362.

38. *Capital*, Vol. I, part I, p. 129. Nevertheless on p. 130 Marx indicates that the "representatives" of gold can be hoarded. But he does not develop the point.

39. *Critique*, pp. 120-121.

40. Knut Wicksell: *Lectures on Political Economy* (London: Routledge, 1934), p. 150.

41. *Capital*, I, 129.

42. Ibid., I, 130.

43. Ibid.

44. Ibid.

45. *Critique*, p. 128.

46. Ibid.

47. *Capital*, I, 134.

48. *Critique*, p. 126. See also my Note 38.

49. *Capital*, I, 133.

50. Ibid.

51. Ibid., I, 113.

52. Ibid., I, 114.

53. Ibid., I, 95-96.

54. *Critique*, p. 105.

55. *Capital*, I, 589.

56. *Critique*, p. 149.

57. Ibid., p. 141.
58. Ibid., p. 146.
59. Ibid.
60. *Capital*, I, 142.
61. Ibid.
62. *Critique*, p. 150.
63. Ibid.
64. Ibid.
65. Ibid.
66. *Capital*, I, 100.
67. Ibid., I, 129.
68. *Contribution to the Critique of Political Economy*, pp. 76-77. In the first case, the state profits as debtor. In the second case, the creditors profit from the operation, but so does the state, as the collector of taxes.
69. Ibid.
70. *Capital*, I, 132.

PART TWO

1. Joseph A. Schumpeter, *History of Economic Analysis* (New York: Oxford University Press), p. 718.
2. See the first volume of *Capital*, Chapter IV, where Marx analyzes "the transformation of money into capital."
3. *Capital*, II, 100.
4. Ibid., II, 358.
5. Ibid., II, 31.
6. Ibid., II, 30.
7. Ibid., II, 117.
8. Ibid., II, 358.
9. Ibid., II, 112-113.
10. I shall not discuss the "period of turnover" so as not to prolong the exposition.
11. *Capital*, II, 354.
12. Ibid.
13. Ibid., II, 30.
14. Ibid., II, 393.
15. Ibid., II, 118.
16. *Capital*, I, 593-598.
17. Ibid., II, 120.
18. Ibid., II, 85.
19. Ibid., II, 120.
20. Ibid., II, 78.
21. Ibid., I, 625 ff. and II, 312 and 333 ff.

22. Cf. *Capital*, II, pp. 364. But this "inflation", like the "deflation" referred to above, is a disequilibrium considered outside the cyclical context.

23. *Capital*, II, 501.

24. Ibid., II, 330.

25. Ibid., II, 333.

26. Ibid., II, 344. See also I, Ch. XXIII, and III, Ch. IV.

27. Ibid. II, 336.

28. Ibid., II, 333.

29. See p. 70.

30. *Capital*, II, 327.

31. Ibid., II, 336.

32. Ibid., II, 491.

33. Ibid., II, 470.

34. *The Accumulation of Capital* (New York: Monthly Review Press, 1964).

35. Ibid., p. 100. Rosa Luxemburg is here faithful to the *letter* of what Marx says. Cf. *Capital*, II, 135-136.

36. Hence the necessity of beginning with Marx's theory of money, cf., First Part.

37. *Capital*, II, 472-473.

38. Ibid., II, 479-480.

39. H. Denis, *Historie de la Pensee économique* (P.U.F., 1966), pp. 426-429.

40. *Capital*, II, 491.

41. Ibid., II, 349.

42. Ibid., II, 347 ff.

43. Ibid., II, 492.

44. Ibid., II, 522-523.

45. Cf. H. Denis, op. cit. It is nevertheless necessary to make clear that Marx here confines himself to the saving of enterprises, or self-financing. Wage-laborers do not save, and their demand for consumption goods is equal to their wages, V (cf. *Capital*, II, 118). But there is sometimes a certain confusion of the terms "saving" and "hoarding" in Vol. II of *Capital*; thus failure of the worker to consume is a saving, that is, Marx makes clear (p. 118), a hoarding, as retention of money corresponding to non-purchase. This is because in the absence of a system of credit, the savings of the laborer cannot be invested.

46. I borrow the terms "pure supply" and "pure demand" from H. Neisser and J.G. Koopmans; in 1933 the latter formulated the equation $M = L$ (that the increase of active money, M, must be equal to that of hoarding), as the condition of equilibrium in terms of the equality of investment and saving. But as I indicate below,

the concept of equilibrium does not have the same meaning in Marx.

47. Paul Sweezy, *The Theory of Capitalist Development* (New York Monthly Review Press, 1968).
48. *Capital*, II, 478.
49. Ibid.
50. Ibid., III, 4.
51. Ibid., II, 116.
52. Ibid.
53. Ibid., II, 413.
54. Ibid., III, 315.
55. Ibid., III, 322.
56. Ibid., III, 317.
57. Ibid., III, 326.
58. Ibid., III, 600.
59. Ibid., III, 593.
60. Ibid., III, 598.
61. Ibid., III, 328.
62. Ibid., III, 325.
63. Karl Marx, *Contribution á la critique de l'économie politique* (Paris: Editions sociales, 1972), p. 181.
64. Ibid., p. 189.
65. Ibid., p. 182.
66. *Capital*, III, 324.
67. Ibid.
68. Ibid., III, 600.
69. Ibid., III, 522.
70. Ibid., III, 479-480.
72. Ibid.
73. Ibid., III, 400.
74. See pp. 77 ff.
75. *Capital*, I, 139.
76. Ibid., I, 137-138.
77. Ibid., III, 479.
78. Ibid., III, 480.
79. Ibid.
80. Ibid.
81. Ibid., III, 401.
82. Ibid., III, 403.
83. *Critique*, pp. 185 ff.
84. *Capital*, III, 458.
85. Ibid.
86. Ibid., III, 425.
87. See pp. 25-26.

88. H. Denis, op. cit., pp. 129-144.
89. In *Lectures on Political Economy*, op. cit., vol. 1, p. 149.
90. Fan Hung, in *The Review of Economic Studies*, vol. 7, No. 1, Oct. 1939.
91. *Capital*, III, 402.
92. Cf. especially Chapter 27 of Volume III, "The Role of Credit in Capitalist Production," where Marx speaks in turn of credit money and stock companies.
93. *Capital*, III, 317-318.
94. Ibid., III, 321.
95. Ibid., III, 436.
96. Ibid., III, 368.
97. Ibid., III, 462.
98. Ibid., III, 544-545.
99. Ibid., III, 545.
100. Ibid., III, 402-403.
101. An altogether different interpretation is given by H. Denis in an article entitled "*Trois théories de l'intérêt du capital*," *Revue économique*, 1950.
102. Article cited. Fan Hung himself makes certain reservations.
103. *Capital*, II, 357.
104. *Capital*, II, 346.
105. Ibid., III, 435.
106. Ibid., III, 370.
107. Ibid., III, 362.
108. Ibid., III, 363.
109. Ibid., III, 356.
110. Ibid., III, 364.
111. Ibid., III, 352-353.
112. Ibid., III, 372.
113. Ibid., III, 509-510.
114. *Critique*, p. 102.
115. *Capital*, III, 344.
116. Ibid., III, 403.
117. Ibid., III, 499.
118. See pp. 66-67.
119. See pp. 68-69.
120. *Capital*, III, 469.
121. Ibid., III, 506.
122. These terms are borrowed by me from the National Accounts.
123. *Capital*, III, 470 and 537.
124. See pp. 80-81.
125. *Capital*, III, 457.
126. Ibid., III, 463.
127. Ibid., III, 466.

128. Ibid., III, 465.
129. Ibid.
130. Ibid., III, 467.
131. Ibid., III, 466.
132. Ibid., III, 467.
133. Ibid.
134. Ibid., III, 469.
135. Ibid.
136. Ibid., III, 502.
137. Ibid., III, 509.
138. Ibid., III, 472.
139. See p. 97.
140. *Capital*, III, 469.
141. Ibid.
142. See first part of this study, pp. 39-40.
143. *Critique*, p. 176.
144. *Capital*, I, 144.
145. See pp. 165 ff. of Ms.
146. *Capital*, I, 143, N.1.
147. *Critique*, p. 177.
148. Ibid., p. 185.
149. Ibid., p. 186.
150. See pp. 87-88. and pp. 108-110.
151. *Capital*, III, 517.
139. Marx's phrase which I quote ends, on the contrary, by saying that the fictitious quality of credit likewise "applies to the 'reserve fund,' where one would at last hope to grasp something solid." But Marx is speaking here of the concentration of the reserves of the private banks in the common funds of the Bank of England, while my comments apply to the banking system as a whole.
152. Ibid., III, 492-493.
153. Ibid., II, 317-318.
154. Ibid., III, 491-492.
155. Ibid., III, 569-570.
156. Marx here takes over the comments of Newmarch, cited in *Capital*, III, 570, No. 15. They are particularly interesting in connection with the present balance of payments difficulties of the U.S.A.
157. This arithmetic concept of devaluation is unfortunately the only one discussed here by Marx.
158. *Capital*, III, 591.
159. Ibid., III, 451.
160. Ibid., III, 567-568.
161. Ibid., III, 517. Thornton had already showed this in 1802.
162. *Capital*, III, 460.
163. Ibid., III, 592.

164. Ibid., III, 581.
165. Ibid., III, 588.
166. H. Bartoli, *La doctrine économique et sociale de Marx, 1950,* p. 221. Cf. also the same author's discussion of Marxist theories on crises in *Fluctuations économiques*, Domat-Monchrestien, 1954 (symposium).
167. *Capital*, III, 304.
168. Ibid., III, 321.
169. Ibid., III, 450.
170. Ibid.
171. Ibid., III, 488.
172. Ibid., III, 489.
173. Ibid.
174. Ibid., III, 178 ff. On this point Marx follows a tradition originating in Cantillon and unknown to Ricardo. Cf. Charles Rist, op. cit., pp. 118-119 and 169.
175. *Capital*, II, 315-316.
176. Ibid., III, 467-468, 480-481, 502, and II, 254-255 and 316.
177. P. Dieterlen, *Quelque enseignements de l'evolution monétaire française de 1948 à 1952,* A. Colin, 1954, p. 82.
178. Ibid., p. 91.
179. See pp. 106-107.
180. *Capital*, III, 569.
181. Ibid., III, 490.
182. Ibid. I, 138, N.1.
183. Ibid., III, 571-572.
184. Ibid., I, 138.
185. *Critique*, p. 146.
186. *Capital*, III, 574.
187. Ibid., III, 254.
188. Ibid., III, 447.
189. See point c) below.
190. *Capital*, III, 458-459.
191. Ibid., III, 530.
192. Ibid., II, 318.
193. Fan Hung, op. cit.
194. *Capital*, I, 122.
195. Ibid., III, Ch. 33.
196. Ibid., III, 541.
197. C. Rist, op. cit., p. 237.
198. *Capital*, III. 403-404, ". . . the principal banks issuing notes . . . actually have the national credit to back them, and their notes are more or less legal tender. . . ."

199. Marx does not discuss in this connection the monetization of the public debt by the central bank and its effect on the politics of monetary control. He only views this financial relationship between the bank and the state as a method of accumulating funds at the expense of the taxpayers. (*Capital*, I, 754 ff.)
200. *Capital*, III, 452.
201. See Part I, p. 47.
202. Capital, III, 543.
203. Ibid., III, 404.
204. Ibid., III, 516-517.

OTHER BOOKS OF INTEREST PUBLISHED BY URIZEN

LITERATURE

Ehrenburg, Ilya
The Life of the Automobile, novel,
   192 pages
Cloth $8.95 / paper $4.95

Enzensberger, Hans Magnus
Mausoleum, poetry, 132 pages
Cloth $10.00 / paper $4.95

Hamburger, Michael
German Poetry 1910-1975, 576 pages
Cloth $17.50 / paper $6.95

Handke, Peter
Nonsense & Happiness, poetry,
   80 pages
Cloth $7.95 / paper $3.95

Hansen, Olaf (Ed.)
*The Radical Will, Randolph Bourne
(Selected Writings) 1911-1918*
   500 pages
Cloth $17.50 / paper $7.95

Innerhofer, Franz
Beautiful Days, novel, 228 pages
Cloth $8.95 / paper $4.95

Kroetz, Franz Xaver
Farmyard & Other Plays, 192 pages
Cloth $12.95 / paper $4.95

Montale, Eugenio
Poet in Our Time (essays), 96 pages
Cloth $5.95 / paper $2.95

Shepard, Sam
*Angel City, Curse of the Starving
   Class, & Other Plays*, 300 pages
Cloth $15.00 / paper $4.95

FILM

Bresson, Robert
Notes on Cinematography, 132 pages
Cloth $6.95 / paper $2.95

Bresson, Robert
The Complete Screenplays, Vol. I,
   400 pages
Cloth $17.50 / paper $6.95

PSYCHOLOGY

Borneman, Ernest (Ed.)
The Psychoanalysis of Money, 420 pages
Cloth $15.00 / paper $5.95

Doerner, Klaus
Madmen and the Bourgeoisie, 384 pages
Cloth $15.00 / paper $5.95

Patrick C. Lee and Robert S. Stewart
Sex Differences, 500 pages
Cloth $17.50 / paper $5.95

Moser, Tilman
Years of Apprenticeship on the Couch,
240 pages / Cloth $10.00

ECONOMICS

De Brunhoff, Suzanne
Marx on Money, 192 pages
Cloth $10.00 / paper $4.95

Linder, Marc
Anti-Samuelson Vol. I, 400 pages
Cloth $15.00 / paper $5.95
Anti-Samuelson, Vol. II, 440 pages
Cloth $15.00 / paper $5.95

SOCIOLOGY

Andrew Arato/Eike Gebhardt (Eds.)
The Essential Frankfurt School Reader,
544 pages / Cloth $17.50 / paper $5.9

Pearce, Frank
Crimes of the Powerful, 176 pages
Paper $4.95

Van Onselen, Charles
Chibaro (African Mine Labor in Southern
Rhodesia), 368 pages / Cloth $17.50

Shaw, Martin
Marxism Versus Sociology
   (A Reading Guide), 120 pages
Cloth $6.95 / paper $2.25

Shaw, Martin
Marxism and Social Science, 125 pages
Paper $2.95

Thönnessen, Werner
The Emancipation of Women, 185 pages
Cloth $10.00 / paper $4.95

Write for a complete catalog to:
Urizen Books, Inc., 66 West Broadway, New York, N.Y. 10007